23·5·07

Primary Science

PGCE Professional Workbooks

Titles in the series:

Professional Issues in Primary Practice
ISBN: 1 903300 65 7
Price: £14

Primary ICT
ISBN: 1 903300 64 9
Price: £14

Primary English
ISBN: 1 903300 61 4
Price: £14

Primary Mathematics
ISBN: 1 903300 62 2
Price: £14

Primary Science
ISBN: 1 903300 63 0
Price: £14

Foundation Stage
ISBN: 1 903300 67 3
Price: £14

To order, please contact our distributors:

Plymbridge Distributors
Estover Road
Plymouth PL6 7PY
Tel: 01752 202301
Fax: 01752 202333
Email: orders@plymbridge.com
www.plymbridge.com

Brenda Keogh, Stuart Naylor,
Max de Bóo and Jayne Barnes

PGCE Professional Workbook

Primary Science

www.learningmatters.co.uk

Concept cartoon on page 6 reproduced from *Thinking About Science*
(Keogh and Naylor, 1997) by kind permission of Millgate House Publishers.

First published in 2002 by Learning Matters Ltd.

British Library Cataloguing in Publication Data
A CIP record for this book is available from the British Library.

ISBN 1 903300 63 0

Cover design by Topics – The Creative Partnership
Project management by Deer Park Productions
Typeset by Sparks Computer Solutions Ltd – www.sparks.co.uk
Printed and bound in Great Britain by Ashford Colour Press, Gosport, Hants

Learning Matters Ltd
58 Wonford Road
Exeter EX2 4LQ
Tel: 01392 215560
Email: info@learningmatters.co.uk
www.learningmatters.co.uk

Contents

Chapter 1:
General Introduction 1

Chapter 2:
Guidance and
Needs Analysis

Introduction 5
Progression in ideas 9
Teaching and learning strategies 13
Teaching practical science 17
Classroom management, organisation and resources 19
Planning and teaching science 22
Children communicating and recording science 27
Assessment and recording in science 31
Other aspects of science education 34
Conclusion 37

Chapter 3:
Getting Started

Introduction 39
Progression in ideas 41
Teaching and learning strategies 43
Teaching practical science 46
Classroom management, organisation and resources 49
Planning and teaching science 51
Children communicating and recording science 54
Assessment and recording in science 57
Other aspects of science education 60
Conclusion 63

Chapter 4:
Developing your
Skills

Introduction 65
Progression in ideas 67
Teaching and learning strategies 70
Teaching practical science 72
Classroom management, organisation and resources 75
Planning and teaching science 78
Children communicating and recording science 82
Assessment and recording in science 85
Other aspects of science education 88
Conclusion 90

Chapter 5:
Extending your Skills

Introduction 91
Progression in ideas 93
Teaching and learning strategies 96
Teaching practical science 98
Classroom management, organisation and resources 101
Planning and teaching science 104
Children communicating and recording science 107
Assessment and recording in science 110
Other aspects of science education 113
Conclusion 116

Chapter 6:
Moving On   117

Bibliography   121
Index   125

Chapter 1   General Introduction

Initial teacher training

Initial teacher training is the start of a continuing process designed to support your professional development throughout your teaching career. This book will support you in identifying strengths and areas for further development in the teaching of science and help you meet the Professional Standards for the award of Qualified Teacher Status (QTS) as set out in *Qualifying to Teach* (DfES/TTA, 2002). These Standards identify what a trainee teacher must know, understand and be able to do in order to be awarded QTS. You will find them listed on the Teacher Training Agency (TTA) website at www.canteach.gov.uk.

There is a variety of different training routes into primary teaching. This book is designed to be flexible enough to support trainees studying on a range of routes, particularly those working on employment-based, flexible, modular or part-time PGCE courses. Trainees on full-time PGCE courses should also find it a useful resource.

Content of the book

The aim of this workbook is to provide you with a framework of activities within which you can develop as a competent teacher of science in a primary school. It does not specifically address the curriculum for Foundation Stage, where science is included within Knowledge and Understanding of the World. However, trainees focusing on this age range should find that the general principles covered in this book will also apply to a nursery or reception setting.

The ideas within the book are grouped within the following themes:

- ➲ progression in ideas;
- ➲ teaching and learning strategies;
- ➲ teaching practical science;
- ➲ classroom management, organisation and resources;
- ➲ planning and teaching science;
- ➲ children communicating and recording science;
- ➲ assessment and recording in science;
- ➲ other aspects of science education.

These are the central issues that you need to understand in order to teach science effectively. There are many more areas that could have been explored. These include your own subject knowledge in science. The Standards for QTS expect you to have 'secure subject knowledge and understanding' of the subjects you are being trained to teach. This book does not attempt to teach you any science directly. However, you will need to make sure that your subject knowledge in science is at a level where you feel competent and confident to recognise and address children's misconceptions and to support learning related to the National Curriculum in Science. You can do this through auditing and developing your own subject knowledge by using resources such as Peacock (1998) or Sharp *et al.* (2002). You might also be directed towards courses and taught sessions by the provider responsible for your training. Your subject knowledge may also be tested as a part of the course.

The expectation on all training courses is that trainees will take some responsibility for developing appropriate knowledge and understanding to enable them to teach effectively. Trainees using this book should draw upon a range of other literature; suggestions for further reading are included to help you with this. Your training provider or other colleagues may recommend additional literature and other resources with which you can enhance your understanding.

We also suggest that you become familiar with the support provided by the Association for Science Education (ASE) at an early stage of the programme. Membership of the organisation is at a reduced rate for trainees. ASE provides access to a wide range of professional development opportunities, high-quality resources and professional expertise. Their web site is www.ase.org.uk.

Structure of the book

In order to recognise the variety of experiences and learning with which trainees start their courses, a flexible needs analysis process is an integral part of this book. You should read through Chapter 2, which is designed to provide an introduction to each of the themes covered in the book. At the end of each theme you will find a linked needs analysis. Detailed guidance on using this can be found on **page 5**. Completing the needs analysis for each theme will help to inform your starting point for learning. In the first instance, however, in discussion with your teacher and training provider, you will need to decide on the best approach to adopt based on the particular training route that you are following.

Once you have read Chapter 2 and completed the needs analysis process, you will have a better idea of your strengths and areas for further development. This will help you to decide where to begin your learning for each theme. It is important to discuss these starting points for learning with your training provider.

The needs analysis will direct you towards school-based activities, which can be carried out in school with different age groups. The activities are grouped in chapters that relate to three stages in your development as a trainee teacher – getting started, developing your skills and extending your skills. The chapters also equate to the types of school experiences that are provided during a PGCE course. The activities will require you to create opportunities to work with groups and classes of children. You will find it helpful to negotiate, at the start of each phase in school, how this will be achieved. You should map out a programme of the activities from this book, and any others that you need to complete, and agree it with your head teacher. This will ensure that you use your time in school effectively and maximise the opportunities that are available to you.

As you complete the appropriate activities in Chapters 3, 4 and 5, you should go back to Chapter 2 and the needs analysis tables to check how you are progressing against the Standards for QTS.

While reading through each chapter, you will come across margin icons that represent key features of the book.

 some further reading

 an example

 a cross-reference

 an activity

Professional Standards for Qualified Teacher Status

By the end of your course, irrespective of the training route followed, you will need to demonstrate that you have met all the Standards required for the award of Qualified Teacher Status. These are generic Standards. You will need to show how these are being applied in the teaching of science.

Evidence of your achievement against the Standards in your science teaching will come from a range of sources. You will need to develop a manageable but comprehensive profiling system that enables you to track your progress against *all* the Standards in different subject areas. It is possible that your training provider will provide you with such a document. You should look carefully at what you are being told about providing evidence. There can a problem with collecting excessive amounts of evidence that do not clearly relate to specific Standards.

It is important that you have a clear view of the difference between completing the activities and providing evidence that you have met the Standards. Evidence gained from completing the activities outlined in this book could be used to demonstrate that you have met *some* of the Standards. The most important sources of evidence of meeting the Standards will include feedback from teachers and tutors, observations of your teaching and final school experience reports, as well as the marking of assignments from your training course. You should share your reflections on the outcomes of activities that you wish to include as evidence with your tutor, mentor or teacher and, where appropriate, ask them to add a comment or to sign your work. A portfolio of the outcomes of the activities and your responses to them will help to chart your professional growth.

We hope you find this book a useful resource to support your training and development as a teacher of primary science. You are beginning a complex and lengthy journey during which you will learn a great deal from a variety of sources, but most especially from the children with whom you have the opportunity to work. They will provide you with the questions that make you want to learn more about scientific ideas; the inspiration to look with them at the world and see some of it as if for the first time; and the insight to know that learning in science should be a journey that you take together.

Chapter 2 Guidance and Needs Analysis ⊃
Introduction

Contents

Introduction	5
Progression in ideas	9
Teaching and learning strategies	13
Teaching practical science	17
Classroom management, organisation and resources	19
Planning and teaching science	22
Children communicating and recording science	27
Assessment and recording in science	31
Other aspects of science education	34
Conclusion	37

This chapter introduces you to the themes that form the strands of development through this book. The themes are:

⊃ progression in ideas;
⊃ teaching and learning strategies;
⊃ teaching practical science;
⊃ classroom management, organisation and resources;
⊃ planning and teaching science;
⊃ children communicating and recording science;
⊃ assessment and recording in science;
⊃ other aspects of science education.

Each of these themes forms an important aspect of becoming an effective teacher of primary science. References for each theme are included in the bibliography.

You can read this chapter as a whole. Alternatively you may choose to select specific themes that you feel are particularly relevant to you at this time. Whichever strategy you choose, if this is the first time that you have read this book then we suggest that you read the classroom story on page 6 first.

How to use the needs analysis tables

After the introduction to each theme, there is a table that allows you to make judgements about your current level of professional development in relation to teaching science. For each table you should look at the statements in the left-hand column. You need to decide which pen portrait provides the best match to your current abilities and experience. Date any that you feel you have already achieved and indicate briefly what evidence you have for making that decision. If you find a column with elements not completed, you should go to the chapter indicated at the bottom of the table. If all the elements are completed then you should move on to the next column. When you have evidence of achievement in all the areas of the needs analysis tables, it is likely that you are close to achieving the Standards for QTS.

The development activities are arranged in three chapters.

Getting Started is a chapter of activities generally aimed at those trainees who have very little or no experience of teaching science. It equates to the very early experience of school that trainees are likely to have at the start of a PGCE course. You may find that, because of limited prior experience, you are at an early stage of developing your understanding of how to teach science. You may be at a different stage in your understanding of the teaching of English or maths.

Developing your Skills is a chapter of activities for those trainees who have spent some time in school. This would equate to a first block of time teaching with whole class responsibility. You are already likely to have worked with groups of children teaching science and are aware of approaches that other teachers use for teaching science.

Extending your Skills is a chapter of activities aimed at those trainees who are becoming confident in their abilities to teach science to a whole class. It equates to a later period of teaching in school, leading to the final assessment against the Standards for QTS. It is assumed that trainees working at this level in the programme will have had a reasonable amount of time working with groups and will have also taught science successfully to whole classes of children. Whatever course you are on and whatever your prior experience, we recommend that you engage in all of the activities in all of the themes in this final stage.

What do we mean by teaching science effectively?

A classroom story

Three children are gathered round a tank of water. They have been discussing their ideas about whether the depth of water will make a difference to how well a boat will float. They each have different ideas.

Concept cartoon of a boat floating on water. © S Naylor and B Keogh.

Now they are enthusiastically beginning to test out their ideas with a variety of boats in a plastic tank of water. They are taking measurements and are recording them in grids that they have drawn in their notebooks.

As far as we can see, the teacher, Mrs Martineau, has only had a brief conversation with the children at the start of the lesson, when she introduced the dilemma of how the boat might float in deeper water using the concept cartoon above. She is now on the other side of the class, apparently uninvolved with the work of some of the groups. The group continues, unaware of the teacher, it seems. They make notes and discuss their conclusions. Some of the children appear to have changed their ideas and one is now very keen to put salt in the water as she thinks this is going to change what happens. The group at the next table, having completed their investigation quickly and being happy about the outcome, are now gathered round the computer, trying to find out more about Plimsoll lines.

Fifteen minutes before the end of the lesson all the children gather together at the front of the class. Each group reports back their findings. Mrs Martineau writes notes on a flip chart in a table that she has drawn in consultation with the children. She doesn't tell them whether they are right or wrong. However, she does seem to encourage questions and generates more discussion about what has happened in the investigations. By the end of the lesson most of the children seem to have agreed on an answer to the question and have concluded that the depth of water does not make any difference as long as the water is deep enough for the boat to float. The Plimsoll line group report back that their enquiry fits in with what everyone has found. The line is not to warn the ship that it is going into deeper water but it is to help avoid overloading the ship.

But there are more questions! Does salt make a difference? Does the shape of the boat matter? Does the number of people in the boat affect the outcome? Mrs Martineau writes them in speech bubbles and puts them on a noticeboard. The only records that the children have made are the jottings in the children's notebooks. Most have created their own format for recording but the group working with the teacher have used grids that they have constructed together with her. Before the end of the lesson the class talk about the usefulness of their data and how each group have decided to record what they found. This generates another discussion. Mrs Martineau leaves her records on the flip chart and tells the children that they will talk more about recording the data tomorrow morning in maths.

Was this really what we were expecting? Where were the instructions for the children to follow? Where was the structured recording using the headings such as apparatus, method and result? How did Mrs Martineau know what most of the children had done? When did the she teach the children the facts about the science? Did she actually know any science or was her lack of knowledge the reason why she left the children to work on their own? Had they learnt anything if they hadn't written the right answer down? Many of the children spent much of the lesson discussing their ideas rather than doing experiments – was this really science?

And yet this felt like a really good lesson. The children could clearly talk about their ideas and obviously understood more at the end of the lesson. They were highly motivated and much of what they did was focused on investigating the issue of floating and sinking.

At the end of the lesson Mrs Martineau talks with you about the lesson and evaluates her practice. She is very pleased with the progress that the children have made. She tells you that she targeted her questions at the children she was less sure about. It confirmed her view that most of the children in the class were really beginning to understand the relationship between forces and floating and sinking. She was pleased that some of the children were thinking hard about the forces involved. She had chosen floating and sinking as an interesting context in which children could explore their growing understanding of forces. Iram and Sally's group had drawn diagrams with arrows showing forces. Sakinna and Toby had used the word 'upthrust' on a diagram, but Mrs Martineau was not certain they really understood what it meant.

Her main concern was about how some of the children had recorded their findings. This had been a target for her lesson. She had hoped that all the children could make their own systematic records and choose the most appropriate means of recording their findings. Clearly some of them were unsure of which approach to use and needed further support. She makes a note against the names of those children she wants to target next time and also records that the children in Iram and Sally's group used arrows to show forces and that Sakinna and Toby have tried to use new language and ideas.

The table below identifies some indicators of good practice. If we review what we have experienced watching this class, which of these criteria have been met? What does this tell us about the lesson? What does it tell us about what you need to learn to be an effective teacher of science in a primary classroom?

Some indicators of good practice
Source: Adapted from Keogh, B. and Naylor, S. *Starting points for science*. Sandbach: Millgate House.

Indicators of good practice in science	Was this illustrated in Mrs Martineau's lesson? How?
A clear sense of purpose to the activity	
Children actively engaged, thinking as well as doing	
Activities are accessible to the children (e.g. language used, concepts involved)	
Activity is responsive to the children's own ideas	
A motivating stimulus for activities	
Teacher uses productive questions which lead on to further enquiry	
A climate of enquiry – children are encouraged to ask their own questions	
Children encouraged to act as independent learners	
Teacher helps the children to learn how to investigate	
Teacher has suitable knowledge of the subject and how to teach it	

Learning to teach science effectively requires a complex blend of understandings, which include your own subject knowledge and knowledge of how to teach science to children. In the following sections we will look more closely at what our teacher needed to know, understand and do in order to achieve a positive outcome with her class.

Chapter 2   Progression in ideas

In this section you will consider the importance of children's own ideas when they are learning science and how understanding this can help teachers to challenge and develop children's ideas. The following key ideas are discussed:

➲ the influences on children's ideas;
➲ what teachers of primary science might understand by the term constructivism and how research into this might influence their teaching;
➲ the importance of the ideas that children hold;
➲ what progression means in primary science;
➲ finding out children's ideas and the value to children and teachers of knowing what these ideas are;
➲ responding to children's ideas;
➲ developing children's ideas.

Teachers used to think that children wouldn't have many ideas of their own in science until they had been taught science. That view has now changed. Now it is widely accepted that children develop firmly held ideas of their own and that these ideas play an important role as they develop their ideas further.

Children's ideas come from a variety of sources. As they interact with the world and gain experience of different events and situations they develop ideas that help them to make sense of the world and how it works. They notice, for example, that when an object is dropped it usually falls to the ground, and they are fascinated by the exceptions to this rule, such as helium balloons or blowing bubbles. Their ideas are also shaped by social interaction and communication. They live in a social world, and their ideas are influenced and shaped by the way that other people make sense of the world in which they live.

Young children will have had limited experience, so inevitably their ideas are restricted. Very often their ideas will be limited to the particular contexts that they have experienced. As they broaden their experience some of their ideas are likely to change. They will probably realise, for example, that not everything that moves is alive. However, many of their ideas are likely to be quite stable. It is quite likely that they will continue to think that all heavy things sink in water and that the moon only comes out at night, for example. What can be surprising for teachers is that children can hang on to their existing ideas very strongly. Even when confronted by experience that seems to be in conflict with their ideas, they do not necessarily change their views. As Harlen (2000, p. 56) notes, '*It is more comfortable to modify an idea than to abandon it, especially if it is your only way of making sense of an observation*'.

Clearly this presents a challenge for teachers. In response to this challenge many teachers adopt a 'constructivist' approach to learning and teaching. Briefly, a constructivist approach recognises that the learner's ideas are important, that these ideas make sense to learners and that they are formed by a process of actively constructing understanding through experience. A useful summary is given in Watt (1998). The task for the teacher is to challenge these existing ideas and to provide experiences that enable learners to construct new and more productive ideas for themselves. Additional guidance on how teachers can use this kind of approach is given in Harlen (2000) and Sharp *et al.* (2000).

How do we recognise when children are developing their ideas? What is the difference between a less well developed idea and a more fully developed idea? The *National Curriculum for Initial Teacher Training* (DfEE, 1998) gives some guidance about how children might progress in science, as shown in the table below. Other authors add to this list. For example, Driver *et al*. (1994) recognise that progress can also mean differentiating existing ideas (e.g. dissolving and melting are separate processes) or integrating existing ideas (e.g. linking separate events in a biological cycle).

Examples of progression in children's understanding of science	
From	**To**
Using everyday language	Increasingly precise use of technical and scientific vocabulary, notation and symbols
Personal scientific knowledge in a few areas	Understanding in a wider range of areas and of links between areas
Describing events and phenomena	Explaining events and phenomena
Explaining phenomena in terms of their own ideas	Explaining phenomena in terms of accepted scientific ideas or models
Participating in practical science activities	Building increasingly abstract models of real situations

Sometimes progression in understanding might consist of a period of consolidation without any shift in the children's ideas. During this period they may be accumulating more experience and developing a more secure understanding. Although this is less obvious it makes a useful contribution to progression. Sometimes progression in understanding might even look like regression. This could happen when children need to set aside one set of firmly held ideas in order to take on a new and more complete understanding of a concept. This often happens to children of primary age when new ideas in one area appear to conflict with those in another. During this period they may appear confused as they reorganise their ideas, but it is often a necessary stage in development.

For example, young children usually have no difficulty with the idea that when you mix two glasses of hot water the water stays the same temperature. As they get older they learn that quantities of different things usually add together. They learn to add money, lengths, volumes, weights, apples, pears and so on. Now when they are asked about what happens when the two glasses of water are mixed they will often say that the water gets hotter. If they are asked to explain their ideas they will use statements such as 'hot water plus hot water equals hotter than hot!' In this case developing their ideas in one area may appear to conflict with what they already know in another area.

It does seem helpful to think of progression in terms of children developing their ideas rather than just in terms of learning new ideas. Ideally it would be good to see this recognised in any Scheme of Work for science, with some guidance about the shift from description to explanation, from small to big ideas, from personal to shared ideas or from concrete to abstract. A Scheme of Work for science should be more than just lists of science concepts that children should learn at different ages and should go on to set out some of the links between these ideas and what progression in understanding means.

Progression is also evident in the skills that children develop as they move from unstructured exploration to more systematic and scientific investigation and enquiry. Harlen (2000) has been influential in describing the links between the skills involved in scientific enquiry and the development of scientific ideas. She points out that when children test out various ideas in order to check whether their existing ideas are adequate, the way that they carry out the tests is crucial. The more highly developed their scientific skills are, the more likely it is that they will reject ideas that don't fit the evidence and accept those that do fit the evidence. Equally, if their skills are not very well developed then they are more likely to ignore contradictory evidence and hold on to their initial ideas even when these don't fit the evidence.

When teachers think about planning for progression in children's ideas it is useful to keep a number of issues in mind.

How should the children's ideas be made evident?
In order to help children's ideas to progress it is helpful if the teacher and the children are aware of what those ideas are. One way to do this is for the teacher to

look at published research. Texts such as Driver *et al.* (1994) or the *Nuffield Primary Science Teachers' Guides* (Collins, 1993) give very useful guidance on what ideas the children are likely to hold. Although texts such as these don't give teachers information about individuals, they can help to provide a good overview of the range of ideas likely to be held in a class.

Teachers can set up situations and activities in which children's ideas will be made evident. It is important not to spend so long exploring the children's ideas that there is no time left to develop them! Some suggestions about appropriate activities are given in the *Nuffield Primary Science Teachers' Guides* (Collins, 1993), including free writing and drawing, structured writing and drawing, completing a picture and discussion with children.

A worthwhile approach is to look for activities that make children's ideas evident and simultaneously begin the process of developing their ideas. This avoids any risk of setting up activities which are only for assessment purposes and which make no contribution to children's learning. Suitable activities include true-false statements, concept maps, sorting and classifying and concept cartoons. More examples of these 'dual purpose' activities are given in Naylor and Keogh (1998). Mrs Martineau in our scenario used concept cartoons. This not only helped her to see the children's initial responses but also gave them a chance to explore their own ideas.

How should I respond to the children's ideas?
Being able to anticipate some of the uncertainties and misconceptions that children may have is useful in planning to develop their ideas. Through becoming aware of the children's ideas the teacher is in a good position to identify areas of uncertainty or confusion and to begin to challenge their ideas. Making the children aware of their own ideas, and the range of ideas in the class, means that they too can be involved in the process of challenging and developing their own and each other's ideas.

One problem is how to respond to the range of ideas that are likely to be present in a typical class. This is compounded by the fact that Schemes of Work may require certain activities so that teachers feel they have very little freedom to respond to the children's individual ideas. There is no easy solution to this dilemma. It can be useful to present activities as problems to be solved rather than as tasks to be carried out, and to emphasise that the purpose of activities is for the children to test out their own ideas in trying to solve the problem. It is also helpful to offer some degree of choice where possible within activities. This helps the children to 'personalise' the activities and see the connection between the activity and their own ideas. Mrs Martineau's children were carrying out similar activities but they had a different sense of purpose depending on their initial ideas. By using such a starting point she was able to give her children some degree of flexibility in how they responded.

How should I help the children to develop their ideas?
New experiences on their own may not be enough to lead to change and development in the children's ideas. It is important to provide problems and challenges that push them into reviewing their own ideas and judging for themselves whether their ideas make sense. It is also important to provide access to alternative ideas that are more scientifically acceptable, for without access to better alternatives the children are very unlikely to discard or modify their initial ideas. Again the *Nuffield Primary Science Teachers' Guides* (Collins, 1993) and Watt (1998) give very useful guidance in this area. Some of the possible approaches listed are:

➲ building on the children's ideas through providing opportunities for them to test out their ideas;
➲ testing the 'right' idea alongside the children's ideas;
➲ modelling imperceptible events;
➲ helping children to generalise from a single context to others;
➲ clarifying children's use of scientific terms.

In the scenario above, Mrs Martineau had not started the lesson by trying to teach the children about floating and sinking. Nor had she started by simply finding out the children's ideas. Instead she had provided a stimulus (the concept cartoon), which presented a problem and led to the children sharing their ideas, helping to clarify for themselves what their initial ideas were and at the same time giving Mrs Martineau access to these ideas. By presenting a problem in a familiar situation she had engaged the children and provided a challenge to all of them about whether the depth of water makes a difference to how the boat floats. Although it was never stated, there was also an implicit challenge to the children to decide what did make a difference to how the boat floated.

As the lesson progressed it was clear that many of the children were progressing from simply describing the situation to being able to explain it; from explaining it in purely personal terms to explaining it in terms of accepted scientific ideas about forces; that some children were using more precise technical vocabulary ('upthrust'); and that some of them were starting to apply their ideas in a wider range of situations. All in all she felt that there was fairly good evidence of progression in the children's scientific ideas during the lesson. This progression had come about by enabling the children to actively construct new ideas for themselves, building on their previous ideas and modifying them where necessary.

Assessing your needs

How far have you developed your understanding of progression in ideas? Reflect on the needs assessment grid below and if possible discuss your ideas with a colleague, teacher or tutor.

Needs assessment: progression in children's ideas

Getting started	Date	Developing your skills	Date	Extending your skills	Date
I have listened to groups of children talking about their scientific ideas		I have tried to make myself aware of the likely misconceptions that children might hold in relation to areas of science that I will be teaching		I understand the importance of researching the misconceptions that children may hold and feel confident to do this for the topics I will be teaching	
When planning to teach a group of children I have thought about the scientific ideas children are likely to hold		When planning for a class of children I have been aware of the need to take children's likely misconceptions in science into account		I understand how to take children's misconceptions into account when planning science lessons	
When teaching a group of children I have tried to make judgements about what scientific ideas the children hold		I have taught a class of children and tried to make judgements about how their scientific ideas are progressing		I understand how to make judgements about children's scientific ideas and how to respond to them through suitable teacher intervention	
I have seen how progression in children's ideas in an area of science is described in a school's Scheme of Work or in the QCA Science Scheme of Work		I have tried to use the progression identified in a Scheme of Work to help me to plan to teach a sequence of lessons in science		I understand how to plan a sequence of lessons to help children's scientific ideas to progress	
If you feel that you have any areas of uncertainty in this column then you should turn to the activities in Getting Started on page 39.		*If you feel that you have any areas of uncertainty in this column then you should turn to the activities in Developing your Skills on page 65.*		*If you feel that you have any areas of uncertainty in this column then you should turn to the activities in Extending your Skills on page 91.*	

Chapter 2   Teaching and learning strategies

The section on teaching and learning will help you to focus on teaching strategies and the likely effect they may have on children's learning. Teachers will often use more than one strategy in a science lesson. The choice of strategy will depend on factors such as the context of the science lesson, safety, resources and time available, your preferences and the children's interests. For example, observing the behaviour of ink drops or food colouring falling into a tall jar of clear water can be taught by teacher demonstration or the children carrying this out themselves in a practical investigation. The explanation for day and night occurring can be demonstrated, modelled, looked up in a book or simulated on a CD-ROM.

In this section you will be considering:

➲ telling/instructing;
➲ demonstration;
➲ differentiating for children with special needs;
➲ children's research using secondary sources;
➲ analogies, models and illustrations (verbal, visual images, 3-D models, drama);
➲ training in the use of scientific/mathematical equipment;
➲ outdoor visits and visitors;
➲ introducing a session;
➲ plenaries;
➲ a role model for science.

Sometimes a well-prepared strategy does not work well due to unpredictable circumstances: the wrong context, classroom interruptions, lack of co-operation from a few disaffected children and so on. Experienced primary teachers are known for their flexibility and will often adapt their approach to the class or individual children when they perceive the need. Whichever strategies you choose, you will need to ensure that in science children will always have some opportunities to carry out practical investigations as well as researching, thinking about and discussing science.

Learning strategies

Children use different strategies to learn (Smith, 1995). The *visual learner* is confident and adept at absorbing ideas and information from text, data and graphs; the *aural learner* remembers ideas and information best when these are spoken aloud by other people or by themselves; the *kinaesthetic learner* learns most effectively when actively engaged in practical activities. Some children are restricted in their performance except when using one particular strategy, while other children learn well using all three strategies.

Reflect on your own preferred learning strategy in science: do you recall or revise best by reading? – by listening or speaking aloud? – or by doing an activity associated with the information you wish to recall? Which of these strategies did you experience when you were learning science? How helpful were they?

When we use a variety of teaching strategies we are able to cater for (differentiate) individual children's learning. For more general background on differentiation, useful references are Dickinson and Wright (1993), NIAS (1995) or Naylor and Keogh (1998).

Identifying teaching strategies for science

Telling/instructing

This strategy, together with *demonstration*, used to be the traditional teaching approach in science. Although we now believe in the importance of children carrying out practical investigations for themselves, this strategy still has its place in science lessons, especially at the start of a lesson to:

⮑ alert children to potential hazards when using tools and equipment (see also Training, below);
⮑ remind children of the appropriate sequence in an enquiry (e.g. close observation before and during investigation);
⮑ remind children about co-operative use of computers, secondary sources, etc.

The strategy is rarely used as the main approach in teaching scientific ideas and cannot, on its own, help children to learn scientific skills.

Demonstration

It would be surprising to see whole lessons in which demonstration is the only teaching strategy employed. However, there may be teachers who like to take a major role in science activities and use a high level of teacher exposition and demonstration in their lessons. They may feel that by limiting the children's opportunity for 'hands-on' activity they are better able to manage the children's behaviour. However, one of the disadvantages of this strategy is that the teacher cannot maintain eye contact with the children when demonstrating. Eye contact is important both for managing behaviour and for involving the children. Some children can feel alienated by continuous demonstration and see little purpose for them in the activity.

Other teachers use demonstration in a more limited way to illustrate points, to engage attention or to enable the children to experience some aspects of science that they could not carry out on their own for reasons such as Health and Safety or limitations on time and resources. Some teachers are cautious of using too much demonstration as they believe that children should experience all science for themselves and that demonstration cannot fully engage all of the children in purposeful activity or encourage them to gain scientific skills. Mrs Martineau, whom we observed above, seemed to take this view in her teaching.

Differentiating for children with special needs

Sometimes we need to make provision for children with individual learning needs (see, for example, BJSE, 1992). Individual provision usually takes place when the whole class or a small group is already engaged in science. The teacher may decide to work with or near the child/children in question or allocate other classroom support, if available. Their learning needs will have been assessed earlier and support may be given through direct intervention, through the use of individualised writing frames or similar written support, another child translating, etc. Children tend to respond well when they perceive the positive efforts the teacher is making for them. Mrs Martineau had noted that some children would have particular problems with recording and had decided that this was where she needed to focus much of her attention.

Children's research using secondary sources

Groups and individuals can pursue science enquiries using books, CDs and websites (ASE's website is a good starting point), and members of their families. Some teachers feel that encouraging children's research is a valuable strategy for developing independent learning and self-esteem, purposeful links between science and ICT, reinforcing home–school links and so on. Some teachers are concerned that independent enquiries may lead to situations where monitoring learning can present difficulties and classroom management is less controllable. Teachers who use this strategy need to identify and ensure good access to resources and help children to be clear about the objectives of their research. Enabling the children to have independent access to such resources can have positive benefits. The children in Mrs Martineau's class who were using the computer to find out about the Plimsoll line were able to work alone and add new information to the whole class discussion.

Analogies, models and illustrations (verbal, visual images, 3-D models, drama)

Science can be problematic, even though it is so stimulating. Many ideas in science seem to contradict common sense (e.g. equal and opposite forces); some scientific processes are invisible (e.g. growth, photosynthesis); and some ideas are just plain difficult to comprehend (e.g. electric current). As teachers, we spend a lot of our time explaining ideas to children and showing them the products of the phenomena as 'proof' that something is happening. Teachers are particularly good at using analogies to explain ideas ('It's like this ... '). We know from research that children not only respond positively to models and analogies but also to the realisation that the teacher is trying to help them understand. This makes models, analogies and illustrations an important teaching strategy (see Asoko and de Boo, 2001, for further guidance).

However, we need to remember that no analogy can show all the features of an idea (for example, comparing electric current with water flowing through a pipe ... electricity can't leak out like water; a torch representing the Sun ... only shows light, and in one direction only). When we use analogies with children, we need to point out the deficiencies of a model as well as what it helps to explain. There are good commercial models available and teachers often make good use of these. Other teachers will use these, and drama, and make their own models. Children respond well to the latter and to invitations to make their own representative models.

Training in the use of scientific/mathematical equipment

Learning to use equipment effectively begins by exposing children to the equipment *before* an investigation takes place, without the pressure of time and accuracy. Lack of confidence or over-confidence in using equipment can lead to unsafe and/or inaccurate measurements. Even with prior experience, children need reminders about safe equipment use and practice before an investigation, such as timing simple walks along the corridor using a stopwatch, measuring the temperature of warm and cold cups of water, or weighing ordinary objects on the digital balance. Some teachers devote time at the start of the science lesson in which the equipment is to be used while other teachers allocate lesson time prior to the science lesson – e.g. during a maths session, in which careful measuring with the equipment is the principal focus.

Outdoor visits and visitors

Outside visits include gardening on the school premises, a trip to the local supermarket, public transport to a museum, a coach trip to the seaside. Visitors to school might include a parent to cook a traditional dish, a representative from the Woodland Trust, a parent working in science or technology or the fire service.

While such visits and visitors can stimulate the start of a science programme, the most effective visits and visitors occur when the children have already had some prior experience of the science focus – e.g. observing the effects of heat on food, a safe demonstration of burning, an investigation of local trees. An outside visit to a museum is much more effective when the children are actively looking for objects or phenomena which they have discussed or explored in the classroom. The children become informed observers. Their attention is already primed and they make better use of the visit/visitor.

Such priming is particularly useful as any outside visitor or visit, even working in the school garden, is an exciting change from regular classwork. This can motivate and stimulate the children's learning but it has implications for classroom management, such as the co-operation needed from the children, guidance for adults who are not familiar to all the children, finding the balance between the science focus and other interests and objectives (e.g. social) and so on.

Introducing a session

While it is acceptable to begin a science session by telling the children what is to be studied, children are more motivated when the introduction includes other stimuli, such as showing the objects to be explored, a story related to the theme of the lesson, a mime of the theme or a big picture for discussion. Mrs Martineau used a concept cartoon (Naylor and Keogh, 2000) as a starting point. This showed the children that there was a range of possible ideas that they should consider and generated productive discussion among the children. The children were keen to find out about their ideas and to carry out investigations and research. Some teachers introduce the science by encouraging the children's questions and noting these down on the whiteboard as reminders and for reflecting upon in the plenary. Some teachers issue a challenge: 'What do you think will happen if ... ' and note down the children's predictions. An introduction that secures the children's attention at the start not only motivates them but also helps to keep their attention during the rest of the science lesson.

Plenaries

As you can see from Mrs Martineau's lesson above, this is an essential part of teaching, whether all the children have been engaged in science or just a few. It is also a productive time for sharing ideas and achievements and for teachers to assess, evaluate and plan the next steps. Teachers plan time for plenaries in their lesson plans. Sometimes the excitement of an investigation carries on right up until the last minute and children are unwilling to 'stop before the bell'. Knowing this can happen, some teachers create a short interval during the practical for mid-lesson feedback and queries and/or allocate time at the beginning of the next lesson for the plenary.

A role model for science

Strictly speaking 'being an enthusiastic and open-minded role model' is not a teaching strategy. However, we know that when we show curiosity and enthusiasm ourselves in the classroom, it is infectious: the children begin to model our attitudes. Apart from encouraging children's effective learning in science, attitudes such as open-mindedness and critical thinking make for good citizens. Science is a wonderful vehicle for acquiring good attitudes so we all need to let children see *our* enthusiasm and curiosity. Mrs Martineau was enthusiastic about the children's ideas. She encouraged them to share ideas and to want to learn more. She willingly shared her own thoughts and added her own questions to those of the children.

Assessing your needs

How far have you developed your understanding of teaching and learning strategies? Reflect on the needs assessment grid below and if possible discuss your ideas with a colleague, teacher or tutor.

Needs assessment: teaching and learning strategies

Getting started	Date	Developing your skills	Date	Extending your skills	Date
I have observed science teaching in a range of different classes and I am aware of some of the strategies that teachers use to teach science		I recognise different strategies that teachers use to teach science. I am aware of how they might vary according to the context and the age of the children		I can use a range of strategies including analogies and models. I can create opportunities for children to engage in purposeful dialogue and be aware of their own ideas and those of other children	
When planning to teach science to a group of children I have thought about the strategies I can use to develop their ideas		When planning to teach science to a class of children I am aware of the need to select appropriate strategies for different forms of enquiry		I can justify my choice of strategies when planning science lessons	
When teaching science to a group of children I have tried different strategies		When teaching science to a class of children I have tried different strategies and am able to evaluate them		When teaching science I can evaluate the success of the strategies I am using and how they affect children's learning	
*If you feel that you have any areas of uncertainty in this column then you should turn to the activities in Getting Started on **page 39**.*		*If you feel that you have any areas of uncertainty in this column then you should turn to the activities in Developing your Skills on **page 65**.*		*If you feel that you have any areas of uncertainty in this column then you should turn to the activities in Extending your Skills on **page 91**.*	

Chapter 2   Teaching practical science

In this theme you will consider some of the specific issues related to teaching practical science, including scientific skills and scientific attitudes.

Scientific skills

The term *practical science* is used here to denote those activities that involve hands-on investigations that are carried out by the children. They form a part of the whole process of finding out about scientific ideas often referred to as scientific enquiry. (DfEE, 1999: 78) Scientific enquiry also includes research involving the use of secondary sources. Practical science encourages and develops the scientific skills (or process skills) described in the National Curricula of England & Wales, Scotland and Northern Ireland. Although the terminology may vary slightly, there is a general agreement that scientific skills comprise: observing and measuring, raising questions, predicting, planning an investigation, collecting data and fair testing, using evidence to draw conclusions, hypothesising or explaining, critical reflection and communication. (See Children communicating and recording science, **page 27**, for details on the last aspect.)

Not all skills will be evident in every practical science lesson and skills are not always used in a linear sequence – for example, observing is a recurring skill. However, there is a recommended structure for an effective science investigation which children learn to use as they develop their scientific skills. Put simply, this involves planning, doing and reviewing. Often the greatest emphasis is on the doing without too much attention being paid to the planning and reviewing parts of the process. In the lesson we observed above, Mrs Martineau had created a situation where her children also needed to plan what they were going to do. The children made different, but appropriate, choices. Mrs Martineau and other teachers in the school had helped them to do this. At the end of the lesson she helped them with the process of reviewing, focusing on drawing conclusions and communicating ideas.

Science has not always been taught through the medium of practical enquiries carried out by the children (Harlen, 1998). The twentieth century saw teaching styles change from didactic teaching and learning by rote, through discovery learning, which allowed children to explore freely, to structured investigations planned by the teacher but carried out by the children. Approaches to practical science are influenced by research, by government guidelines and constraints, by time limitations and by the personal preferences of the teacher. While individual teachers may vary in their use of practical science activities, there is a consensus that, on their own, neither didactic teaching nor random discovery learning are likely to enable children to acquire a good foundation of scientific skills and knowledge. Children do need opportunities to explore but set within a programme that includes structured scientific enquiries targeting specific scientific concepts.

The emphasis on process skills stems from the belief that science is not simply a body of knowledge but a way of behaving systematically, a way of perceiving and responding to questions or unfamiliar phenomena (Ratcliffe, 1998). Systematic practical investigations reduce the risk of 'jumping to conclusions' without support for these conclusions. The scientific process is a method of challenging assumptions, speculation and prejudice. We need to teach children how to think critically and science is one of the best vehicles for acquiring this skill. Needless to say, science can sometimes give us the 'wrong' answers, so we need to be critical about scientific generalisations too!

Not all scientific enquiry involves some kind of practical investigation. This is particularly true when studying living things and the environment, when other types of enquiry methods are frequently needed. Scientific enquiry can include looking for patterns (such as where a particular type of flower is found), classifying things (e.g. recognising insects) and solving problems (e.g. measuring the strength of a magnet). However the most common and the most recognisable type of scientific enquiry is fair testing. In a fair test one factor is changed and the effect on another factor is measured. For example, you might look at the effect of stirring on how quickly salt dissolves in water by stirring for 10, 20 or 30 seconds or not at all. In a fair test all the other factors should be kept the same, apart from the one you are changing and the one you are measuring. In the example with salt dissolving in water you would need to keep the temperature, the amount of water and the amount of salt the same otherwise the test would not be fair.

Children will not discover how to carry out scientific enquiries without being shown. It is important that teachers model good enquiries with children, that they discuss in advance how an enquiry might be carried out, that they look back and evaluate scientific enquiries and that they discuss with the children what makes the difference between a good and a poor scientific enquiry. In this way children will come to recognise what a scientific enquiry looks like and learn how to carry these out themselves.

Scientific attitudes

Practical scientific enquiries help children to develop attitudes that will empower them as learners and as future citizens (Harlen, 2000). These attitudes are not exclusive to science but it is easy to see how they can be developed alongside process skills. Scientific attitudes include: curiosity, open-mindedness, willingness to tolerate uncertainty, creativity and inventiveness, perseverance, respect for evidence, critical awareness and co-operative teamwork. At the end of the lesson Mrs Martineau showed that there were still questions to be answered, even though some answers had been found, reinforcing the view that science is about questions and not just answers.

Assessing your needs

How far have you developed your understanding of teaching practical science? Reflect on the needs assessment grid below and if possible discuss your ideas with a colleague, teacher or tutor.

Needs assessment: teaching practical science					
Getting started	**Date**	**Developing your skills**	**Date**	**Extending your skills**	**Date**
I have observed teachers teaching practical science		I am aware of the difference between developing practical skills and developing conceptual understanding in science		My teaching encourages children to make independent decisions about the scientific activities in which they are engaged	
When planning to teach a group I have thought about how to develop their practical skills in science		When planning for a class I have considered issues relating to teaching practical skills in science		I can use a range of strategies to help children to develop their practical skills and make judgements about their learning	
I have looked at a school's Scheme of Work, the QCA Scheme of Work and resources to support the teaching of practical skills		I have taught science to a class of children and reviewed their engagement in practical activity		I can evaluate the effectiveness of my teaching in relation to children learning practical skills	
If you feel that you have any areas of uncertainty in this column then you should turn to the activities in Getting Started on **page 39**.		*If you feel that you have any areas of uncertainty in this column then you should turn to the activities in Developing your Skills on* **page 65**.		*If you feel that you have any areas of uncertainty in this column then you should turn to the activities in Extending your Skills on* **page 91**.	

Chapter 2   Classroom management, organisation and resources

We will now consider how you make the classroom work effectively for teaching science. There is a strong overlap between this section and the two previous sections.

Managing science in the primary classroom is underpinned by the same guiding principles that support all effective teaching of primary age children. These are explored in Waterson (2000) or Sharp *et al.* (2002), Chapter 7. There are some organisational issues that are particularly significant in ensuring that children gain a safe and purposeful experience in science. As a teacher you will need to make decisions about these issues according to what you wish to achieve with the children and the context in which you are working.

In this section you will consider:

⊃ whole class involvement;
⊃ small group activities;
⊃ groupings for science;
⊃ classroom layout;
⊃ organisation of resources;
⊃ health and safety.

Whole class involvement

Sometimes teachers feel that it is appropriate to have the whole class engaged in science activities at the same time, to share ideas and to create an atmosphere of purposeful enquiry. Some teachers are concerned that this may lead to a situation that they will find more difficult to manage. They believe that whole class activity can stretch resources and behaviour may be difficult to control. However, whole class activity does not necessarily mean all the children investigating at the same time. Some children might be carrying out research using secondary sources. Normally children who are used to working in this way are unlikely to be problematic. This was evident in Mrs Martineau's class.

The teacher needs to consider which role to take in supporting the activity – for example, focusing on a small number of children and allowing other groups to work independently. This was the decision that Mrs Martineau took. She spent much of the time with one group, although she did occasionally intervene with other groups to manage the class effectively. Her class have learnt how to work effectively on their own. The teaching strategies that she used in the lesson gave the children a clear sense of purpose and presented a manageable way of organising whole class activity. An alternative role is for the teacher to move around the room, intervening where it seems appropriate.

In some cases, all the children may carry out identical investigations and, although this gives less scope for individual group motivation, it is possible to have a tight focus on the targeted concept and skill in the plenary. On other occasions groups will be investigating different aspects of the same focus (e.g. comparing one ball bouncing on different surfaces/comparing different balls bouncing on one surface, etc). In this case the plenary would refer to a range of related concepts, which can be very motivating for children.

Small group activity

This is a strategy often used in Key Stage 1 classes. A small group of children will be carrying out a science activity while the rest of the class work on other curriculum areas. The children may be working unsupported by an adult, independently exploring their ideas. On other occasions, the teacher or other adult may focus on the science group. Some teachers feel that it is important to stay with the group doing science as they may miss some important ideas. Others feel that the opportunity for children to explore phenomena on their own is an essential part of learning in science. Both of these strategies are important if children are to have structured support to develop their skills and learn to work independently. Whichever role the teacher adopts, this strategy will need opportunities for children to share their learning.

Groupings for science

When the decision is to work with groups for all or part of the lesson then the teacher will decide which kind of grouping to use when planning the lesson.

What kinds of grouping can be used?

➲ **Grouping by ability in literacy or numeracy.** Often the choice is to use literacy or numeracy groupings as these are the most predominant groupings in most classes. Grouping like this may help the teacher to provide science experiences where the mathematical or linguistic challenge is appropriate for the children. However, there is not always a direct relationship between scientific ability and ability in other areas. Sometimes there is a mismatch between the mathematical or linguistic demand in an activity and the scientific demand.

➲ **Grouping by scientific ideas.** You will notice that some teachers will try to put children with similar ideas together. This could be helpful if the teacher wants to target a particular misconception with some children. However, evidence from research shows that children tend to learn more effectively if a group contains children with a range of ideas (Howe, 1995).

➲ **Grouping by separate genders or prescribed gender mix.** In some classes the teacher may have decided that gender is a significant issue in the way that children are grouped for science. There is some evidence that there are differences in the way girls and boys perform and behave in science lessons. Some teachers are concerned that boys may dominate groups or that different kinds of scientific activities appeal to girls and boys (Sjoberg, 2000). Others may think having a mix of girls and boys brings balance to the groups.

Mrs Martineau chose to use groups for most of the lesson. The groups were of mixed ideas and gender but she had drawn together a small group of four children whom she knew were likely to struggle with the recording based on her knowledge of their mathematical ability. You will need to make decisions about grouping based on your knowledge of how children learn most effectively in your class.

Classroom layout

Classroom layout can have a significant effect on the way in which children are able to respond to lessons and engage in learning. You can find out more about classroom layout in Waterson (2000) or Sharp *et al.* (2000).

➲ Classrooms arranged in rows may limit group discussion, could restrict movement and therefore the children's autonomy, but could allow pairs of children to work closely and effectively together. It is unusual to see science taught in rows unless a low priority is being given to scientific investigations and group discussion.

➲ Some clustering of desks, if poorly planned or in a room that is too small for such an arrangement, can similarly restrict movement and make carrying out practical work stressful for the teacher and children, particularly where access to resources is restricted. However, clustering desks can also be used to enhance group work, allowing the sharing of ideas and materials and utilising larger desk areas for practical activity.

Organisation of resources

The way that children access resources for science could reveal a lot about the teacher's view of the children as independent scientific enquirers. It is possible for children aged 5 and younger to manage their own resources, making decisions about what equipment may be needed at any particular time to extend their activities and their ideas. Some teachers like to feel in more direct control of the way children collect and use resources. However, independence and making decisions about appropriate resources are key aspects of learning to work scientifically (DfEE, 1998: 83). Classrooms will vary in the way that science resources, computer programmes and books are organised. You should look for the child-friendliness of labelling, the accessibility of resources for all children, the amount of involvement of the children in organising resources, discussion about resources and so on. Feasey (1998) gives useful guidance about resources.

You could see by the way that the children set up their own investigations and moved freely from investigating to using the computer that Mrs Martineau had created an environment that supported children's independent work and allowed free access to sources of information.

Health and Safety

In all aspects of teaching you need to consider Health and Safety issues. We cannot assume that because it is science it is always dangerous. However, science has potentially more safety issues than some subjects and there are some aspects of science that can be more hazardous than others. The use of candles or heating elements has obvious dangers, but there are also hazards involved in activities that do not appear to be so problematic. You may find that there are specific restrictions within the school or that the local authority has issued subject-related guidelines. Before each lesson it is appropriate to carry out a risk assessment even if you think that the risk will be minimal. The *Be Safe* book (2001) from the Association for Science Education is essential reading when planning science.

Assessing your needs

How far have you developed your understanding of classroom management, organisation and resources? Reflect on the needs assessment grid below and if possible discuss your ideas with a colleague, teacher or tutor.

Needs assessment: classroom management, organisation and resources					
Getting started	**Date**	**Developing your skills**	**Date**	**Extending your skills**	**Date**
I have learnt about organising science by observing other teachers in different age groups		I understand the different kinds of organisational strategies that can be used for practical work and for other kinds of scientific enquiry		I understand how organisational strategies can be context-related	
I have talked to teachers about their organisation for science		When planning for a class of children I have been able to choose different kinds of organisation		I understand that effective teachers use a wide range of organisational strategies and recognise the reasons for their choices	
I have made judgements about the effectiveness of different approaches to classroom management		I have evaluated the organisational strategies that I use in my teaching		I have modified my organisation through evaluation and research into classroom organisation	
I am aware that Health and Safety is an important consideration when planning for science		I have taken Health and Safety issues into account in my planning		I take account of Safety policy and practice in my teaching	
*If you feel that you have any areas of uncertainty in this column then you should turn to the activities in Getting Started on **page 39**.*		*If you feel that you have any areas of uncertainty in this column then you should turn to the activities in Developing your Skills on **page 65**.*		*If you feel that you have any areas of uncertainty in this column then you should turn to the activities in Extending your Skills on **page 91**.*	

Chapter 2   Planning and teaching science

In this theme you will consider planning for science and thinking about how to make it effective. Although you may have considered planning in the context of other curriculum areas there are some specific issues to look at in science, particularly as many lessons will include practical activities. You will find that many schools use different planning structures for different subjects. In English and maths the National Strategy documents provide some guidance for planning. The science documentation does not offer such guidance.

In this section you will consider:

⊃ the National Curriculum for science;
⊃ Schemes of Work;
⊃ long- and medium-term planning;
⊃ lesson plans – (or short-term plans) and how to make them effective.

The National Curriculum for science

The science planning in a school will be based on the National Curriculum for Science document (DfEE, 1999). You should have the document available when reading this section.

The National Curriculum sets out the teaching requirements for children in different Key Stages through a Programme of Study. If you turn to pages 78–89 in the document you will see that the Programme of Study for science is divided into four areas and you need to be familiar with these.

⊃ Science 1 (Sc 1) or Scientific Enquiry is concerned with (i) Ideas and Evidence in Science and (ii) Investigative Skills.
⊃ Science 2 (Sc 2) is the section on Life and Living Processes (essentially biology).
⊃ Science 3 (Sc 3) is Materials and their Properties (essentially chemistry).
⊃ Science 4 (Sc 4) is Physical Processes (essentially physics).

You may find it helpful to remember that these are listed in alphabetical order – biology, chemistry, physics.

There are two Programmes of Study, one for Key Stage 1 and one for Key Stage 2. You will find that there are themes running through the two Key Stages that the children will revisit at different levels so that their ideas are helped to progress.

Sc 1 or Scientific Enquiry underpins the other areas of science. The National Curriculum states, *'Teaching should ensure that scientific enquiry is taught through contexts taken from the sections on Life and Living Processes, Materials and their Properties and Physical Processes'* (DfEE, 1999: 78). When identifying learning objectives for planning lessons you should always try to consider Sc 1 objectives as well as those from Sc 2, 3 or 4.

Look at the document and use it to try to decide which parts of it Mrs Martineau used to plan her teaching. You should easily be able to find reference to the skills that she was developing but where does floating and sinking come in? Which parts of the Programme of Study do they come from? Can you also identify what the children might have learnt earlier to map the possible progression of their ideas from Key Stage 1?

Planning and teaching in a school is supported by a series of documents. These may vary from school to school but typically include the following:

- ⊃ whole school policy;
- ⊃ whole school/dept. guidelines;
- ⊃ whole school/dept. Scheme of Work;
- ⊃ class year plan;
- ⊃ class term plans;
- ⊃ class weekly plans;
- ⊃ class daily plans.

The policy sets out the general aims for science in the school. Normally it will reflect the National Curriculum expectations and the school's own philosophy and beliefs about teaching science.

The guidelines show how the policy will be interpreted in practice and provide help for the development of the Scheme of Work. For example if the policy states that children's ideas should be recognised in science then the guidelines will provide exemplification of a range of strategies for putting this aim into practice.

Schemes of Work

The Scheme of Work will be drawn up using the guidelines, the National Curriculum for science and other material. It will map out the science curriculum in some detail across every age range in the whole school. The Qualification and Curriculum Authority (QCA) has produced a Scheme of Work for science (QCA, 1998) to support schools' planning. It is a non-statutory document that translates the NC requirements into a practical plan. Many schools use this Scheme of Work as the basis for their planning. While it provides guidance, some schools feel that they need to develop it further to reflect their own context and make it relevant to the children in the school. Other schools will integrate the ideas from the QCA document with materials from a commercial Scheme of Work. Some will just use a commercial scheme and yet others will have developed their own.

Some Schemes of Work are accompanied by support materials such as work sheets and children's books. Some are very extensive, providing substantial detail about what can be taught to children across the whole school. It is unlikely that any one scheme will meet all the needs of the school. It is important that you learn at an early stage to look critically at such resources.

You should familiarise yourself with these documents when you are starting to teach in a new school.

Long- and medium-term planning

When you go into a school you are likely to be presented with planning that has already been agreed by the staff. Often you will be given the termly map of the work to be covered (medium-term plan) although the school may wish to involve you in this process. Sometimes you will also receive a more general overview that provides a sense of where your teaching will fit into the science teaching for the whole year or Key Stage (long-term planning). It is not unusual for trainees to be given the section of the QCA Scheme of Work to work from. If this is the case, you should consider how purposeful the activities would be for the children in your class. Is there any way in which you can bring the ideas alive and make them more relevant for them?

The medium-term planning is likely to identify the key learning objectives, teaching activities and learning outcomes, along with other information such as vocabulary, resources and key questions. It would be normal for you to annotate and develop the plans that you are given as long as you retain the learning objectives for the class for that period of time. It is from this detailed overview that teachers plan individual lessons or groups of lessons. The QCA Scheme of Work and suggested teaching activities are *not* detailed individual lesson plans.

Lesson plans

Good lesson plans in science, as in any other subject, should start with the learning objectives, not the activity. You need to identify what the children will be expected to learn and plan the activities around these objectives. You should not have too many – two or three learning objectives should be the focus for the lesson. For example, these are Mrs Martineau's objectives:

By the end of the lesson:
Most children:
➲ *will have consolidated their understanding of how to carry out an independent investigation;*
➲ *will have increased their understanding of how to choose independently an appropriate way of recording their findings (applying new learning about recording data from previous maths lessons);*
➲ *will have consolidated their understanding of forces in the context of floating and sinking.*

Joelle, Kamu, Ceri and Craig:
➲ *will have increased their understanding of recording their findings in charts so that they are more effective at making decisions about which will be most appropriate.*

You will now know that the first two learning objectives are investigative skills (taken from Sc 1 – Scientific Enquiry) and the last one is about concepts (from Sc 4 – Physical Processes). Good science planning and teaching will try to identify Sc 1 learning objectives, as well as those from the other areas of study, whenever possible.

When planning science lessons you will need to consider carefully how you will create the balance between the need to develop procedural understanding and practical skills and the need to develop conceptual understanding. There is evidence that children find it difficult to develop both at the same time and that it is better to focus on one or the other. Look at Mrs Martineau's objectives: can you decide whether she is focusing on procedures or concepts? Can you see how this varies subtly between the whole class and the small group and how important the word independent is in this context?

Lesson plans will often be written in a particular format, depending on the school that you are in. Look at Mrs Matineau's whole lesson plan on **page 25**. What are the key headings in the plan? Can you see how questions and awareness of possible misconceptions are part of her planning? How has she organised her lesson to take the children's own ideas into account? Can you see how she has identified her role and that of the children? In which ways has she differentiated the work to provide support for some children and challenge for others? As a trainee it is important that you consider all these aspects of planning the lesson.

It is advisable to create a list of headings so that you can either produce your own structure or amend a school's plan where necessary. It may be useful to put a planning pro forma on your computer and then you can write in the details, expanding spaces where necessary. This type of planning format is also described in Sharp *et al.* (2002: 57–9).

LESSON PLAN	
Subject: science	**NC ref:** Sc 1; Sc 4 2d

Date: 11 October	**Duration:** 1.5 hrs	**Class:** Year 6	**Number of children:** 29

Main purpose of the lesson
Scientific enquiry – the whole process of an investigation from planning through to obtaining and considering evidence (Sc 1). Some children using secondary sources

Scientific context
Forces – opposing forces (context floating and sinking – not in the NC but enjoyable and builds on previous work – good context for applying ideas about forces – an opportunity to extend more able children) (Sc 4 2d)

Children's previous experiences
All children planned, carried out and evaluated in science. Most independent but need to consolidate their skills. They are willing to share their ideas. All of them need to think more about recording their investigation. All carried out work on forces and explored floating and sinking in KS 1 and last week

Lesson outcomes	**Learning objectives**
All children will have: • engaged in discussion about a scientific idea (floating and sinking) • planned, carried out and reviewed a scientific investigation • drawn conclusions • recorded their findings (some with support) Some children will have: • used secondary sources (computer and books) • explored new language introduced to them last week	By the end of the lesson: Most children: • will have consolidated their understanding of how to carry out an independent investigation • will be able to choose an appropriate way of recording their findings • will have increased their understanding of forces in the context of floating and sinking Joelle, Kamu, Ceri and Craig: • will have increased their understanding of recording their findings

Lesson sequence

Intro **Recap last lesson (15 mins)** • Discuss ways that we explored our ideas and how we used charts and notes to record our findings (share examples) • Explore their ideas about how we plan and carry out investigations • Remind class about the computer and books • Introduce the concept cartoon • remind them that it doesn't matter what ideas they have	**Child activity (40 mins plus 10 tidying up)** *Most groups:* • Work in same small groups as last week (list on the noticeboard) • Each group to spend some time discussing their ideas about the concept cartoon • Get some brief feedback after 10 mins • Children to organise their own investigation and to record findings • They can use secondary sources as extension *Focus group:* • Allow them some time to discuss on their own • Monitor their activity and join them when they are beginning to plan to ensure that recording is part of their thinking • Provide structured support for their recording but let them explore ideas on their own	**Plenary (evaluation) (20mins)** Identify key ideas from each group: • What did they find? Did they change their minds? • Do we all agree? • Identify any questions that are remaining – put on the question board in speech bubbles • How did they record? What did they record? • Feedback from target group on their recording • Evaluate recording strategies • Put results on whole class recording sheet to reinforce recording strategy

Differentiation Support – see focus group above Some differentiation by outcome Extension – computer-based research and presentation; use of secondary sources	**Assessment** Focus on recording strategies – monitor during the lesson and look in the books Note any significant progress in understanding forces but not main target Monitor their effectiveness in carrying out a whole investigation	**Homework** Ask at home what other people think – bring ideas in for tomorrow afternoon's follow-up session	**Resources** Tanks Plastic boats Centicubes (children can access other resources themselves)

Safety Children carrying tanks of water Spilt water to be cleared up straightaway	**ICT** Research using Internet

Mrs Martineau's lesson plan

Assessing your needs

How far have you developed your understanding of planning science? Reflect on the needs assessment grid below and if possible discuss your ideas with a colleague, teacher or tutor.

Needs assessment: planning science					
Getting started	**Date**	**Developing your skills**	**Date**	**Extending your skills**	**Date**
I have seen examples of teachers' plans for science		I am aware of the strategies used by teachers to differentiate science activities		I understand how to use assessment to produce plans for teaching science that match children's needs	
I can construct a plan for teaching science to a small group using a pro forma provided for me		I know how to plan for teaching science to a class using both medium- and short-term plans		I understand the different levels of planning for science and how to construct them	
I can recognise when a plan for a science lesson is well structured		I have begun to evaluate my science plans and to understand what makes planning effective		I evaluate selected aspects of my planning in order to improve it	
I have used the QCA Scheme of Work and the National Curriculum to help with my planning		I use suggestions from the QCA Scheme of Work or elsewhere to provide activities for children		My plans are comprehensive, with clear learning objectives and purposeful and motivating activities	
*If you feel that you have any areas of uncertainty in this column then you should turn to the activities in Getting Started on **page 39**.*		*If you feel that you have any areas of uncertainty in this column then you should turn to the activities in Developing your Skills on **page 65**.*		*If you feel that you have any areas of uncertainty in this column then you should turn to the activities in Extending your Skills on **page 91**.*	

Chapter 2 Children communicating and recording science

In this section you will look more closely at issues to do with children communicating their own ideas in science. This is often an area that is not fully developed by teachers, and at times children may not have the skills to communicate science at a level that is appropriate for their age and ability.

In this section you will consider:

⮞ children's use of scientific terminology;
⮞ children's drawings;
⮞ how children record and communicate their ideas;
⮞ literacy, numeracy and science.

The National Curriculum for science at Key Stage 1 states that children *share their ideas and communicate them using scientific language, drawings, charts and tables* (DfEE, 1999a: 78), and at Key Stage 2, *'communicate ideas using a wide range of scientific language, conventional diagrams, charts and graphs'* (DfEE, 1999a: 83).

Children's use of scientific terminology

One of the ways in which progression in science learning is recognised is the progress from using everyday language to increasingly precise use of technical and scientific vocabulary, notation and symbols (QCA, 1998).

Children talk about science from a very early age. However, their early scientific language might limit the way that they can convey their ideas, both orally and in writing. Here are some examples of what five-year-old children have said when talking in science lessons:

The window is all muddied up (condensation).
The water has disappeared (evaporation).
I can make rain (sand pouring through a sieve).
There are colours painted on the sky (a rainbow).
How do you get bigger? You just do!
The sandcastle has melted.

Do these sentences mean that the children understand very little about science? These early explanations and statements are important for children developing their conceptual understanding. We cannot always be certain what a child understands from what they say. All learners have to explain the world in language that they know. Sometimes language does not keep pace with the child's developing ideas and their observations. At other times they will try out new terminology but will not have a precise enough meaning to use it accurately, as in the above example of the sandcastle melting.

The teacher's role is to encourage children to explore their scientific ideas in whatever language they have available to them. It is also to help them to try out new terminology and to give it increasing explanatory power through discussing ideas, through modelling its correct use and through experiencing related phenomena. Some teachers are reluctant to introduce new terminology to children too early in case they get it wrong. Many others feel that if children are not given the opportunity to experiment with scientific language they will not have the terminology available to support the development of their scientific concepts.

In order for children to develop confidence in using scientific terminology they need to:

➲ play with scientific language as a part of science lessons;
➲ talk about scientific terms and related concepts when they observe phenomena;
➲ hear explanations of scientific terms;
➲ see scientific terminology around the classroom;
➲ talk about scientific ideas in whatever language feels appropriate, including their first language if they are bilingual;
➲ work with classroom and language assistants who are aware of the likely scientific terms that will be used in a particular lesson.

Children's drawings

Drawing can be a very useful means of enabling children to communicate their ideas, especially when they are annotated. They also provide a tangible record of children's thinking, which can be useful as evidence of their achievement as part of a portfolio of work in science.

Drawings are made more valuable if children are asked to draw what they think is happening rather than simply what they see (Harlen, 2000). For example, children looking at evaporation from a tank of water could be asked to simply draw the water level in the tank before and after it had evaporated, but it would be more valuable to invite them to draw what they think made the water level go down. Including explanation rather than just description in their drawings enables them to communicate their ideas more effectively.

Drawings can also be predictive. For example, children can be asked to draw what they think a large block of ice will look like in an hour and in a day's time, or to draw what they think will happen to potato peelings on a compost heap. In the scenario described earlier Mrs Martineau could have asked the children to draw what they thought would happen to the boat when the water in the tank was deeper. This would have enabled the children to communicate their ideas, given the teacher access to their ideas and also helped to clarify the children's thinking before they engaged in any kind of investigation. If they were to produce a second drawing after their investigations to show why they think the boat floats the way it does then that would be even more valuable. It would enable the children to communicate their ideas about the factors involved in floating and sinking and help them to become more aware of their own learning.

As with spoken language, it is important to recognise the limitations on children's communication through drawings. Children may not always have the motor skills to produce accurate records of their ideas. Also children need to learn how to use careful observation in their drawings and to recognise the differences between an artistic and scientific representation of their ideas. It is not surprising to find children using artistic representation of their ideas if this has been encouraged in other parts their work in the classroom.

How children record and communicate their ideas

In the classroom we observed earlier, Mrs Martineau was focusing on the children's ability to record and communicate. There are a number of useful questions to ask about children recording their science ideas and findings:

➲ Why are the children recording their results?
➲ Who are they recording for? Are they communicating their ideas to anybody?
➲ Is a range of recording strategies used?
➲ Do the children always record individually?
➲ Does the recording method influence how the children collect results?
➲ Do the children make use of ICT in recording and communicating?
➲ Would there be any advantage in using data loggers to help children collect data?

The impact of the Literacy Hour has led to an increased use of writing frames to support children's writing. These have also been used for some time in science as a means of helping children to plan and record their investigations. Although these are extremely valuable there is some risk that they can be over-used, so that children come to see science as a short hands-on activity followed by a lengthy and laborious write-up. There are a range of imaginative ways of getting the children to record and communicate their learning in science so that this does not become too much of a routine (Burton, 1995). These include annotated drawings, 'comic strip' sequences, class displays, information leaflets, posters, letters and advertisements. Many of these alternative approaches present valuable opportunities for linking science with literacy. They all help children to personalise their recording and emphasise that the purpose of making a record is to communicate with others.

The use of ICT also offers some potentially valuable ways in which children can record, present and communicate their results in science. The National Curriculum identifies the need to use information and communication technology across the curriculum (DfEE, 1999: 78, 83) and this is especially relevant in science, both for collection of data and communicating findings. ICT can be used *as a tool to handle and process information, to measure, to communicate and to model their ideas to help answer their questions* (Ball, 1998: 168). Sharp *et al.* (2002) give further background on the use of ICT in science.

Literacy, numeracy and science

As the curriculum has become more focused on literacy and numeracy, other core and foundation subjects have had less time allocated to them. One way round this potential problem is to try to link science and literacy together so that each supports the other, with science providing a meaningful context for using literacy skills (Feasey, 1998). For example, the focus for many literacy lessons is the use of non-fiction books. Why not use science books for this? Although the learning objectives may be focussed on the text and how it conveys meaning, rather than on developing scientific concepts, this can be a valuable opportunity to extend the children's science learning or as a lead in to later scientific enquiry. Similarly, when children are writing they could be writing about something scientific. It could be writing a set of instructions for carrying out an investigation, a poem about the appearance of grains of salt under a microscope or producing a dictionary of scientific terms. Using curriculum time in this way allows you to cover two subjects at the same time.

Of course, science also has its own literacy, its own vocabulary and its own genres or styles of text. To develop expertise in science it is necessary for children to have at least some knowledge of these. For example, certain styles of writing (such as explanation texts and instructional writing) are particularly common in science, and children can be helped to see the value of these. First Steps (1998) is helpful in identifying these different genres and suggesting contexts for their use.

When considering science and numeracy you will find that many of the skills taught in mathematics are exactly the skills that children require for recording and communicating results in science. This applies particularly to the skills involved in data handling. The framework for teaching mathematics, when making links between mathematics and other subjects, states that:

Almost every scientific investigation or experiment is likely to require one or more of the mathematical skills of classifying, counting, measuring, calculating, estimating and recording in tables and graphs. In science pupils will, for example, order numbers, including decimals, calculate simple means and percentages, use negative numbers when taking temperatures, decide whether it is appropriate to use a line graph or bar chart, and plot, interpret and predict from graphs. (DfEE, 1999b: 17)

Some of these skills are part of the process of investigating in science as well as part of the process of handling data. When the skills overlap like this it is possible to view a science lesson as contributing to learning in maths and vice versa.

Science can also provide a meaningful context for teaching mathematical skills (Feasey and Gallear, 2000). As in the case of literacy, using a science focus can allow you to teach the maths lesson you would have taught anyway, but to teach it from a different perspective. The science focus makes the mathematics purposeful for the children. It also helps the children's understanding of the science involved.

Assessing your needs

How far have you developed your understanding of communicating and recording science? Reflect on the needs assessment grid below and if possible discuss your ideas with a colleague, teacher or tutor.

Needs assessment: communicating and recording science					
Getting started	**Date**	**Developing your skills**	**Date**	**Extending your skills**	**Date**
I have listened to groups of children using scientific terminology		I am aware of how ICT can be used to record the results of scientific enquiry		I use ICT to help children record the results of scientific enquiry	
When planning to teach a group I consider how they will record and communicate the results of their learning		I can select from a range of methods to record results when teaching science to a class		I understand how to build links between numeracy and teaching science	
I have looked at examples of children's recording in science		I have evaluated a range of recording strategies and can decide which strategies are suitable for which purpose		I understand how to build links between literacy and teaching science	
I have observed the way that children communicate their results in science		I am aware of how to help children to develop their recording and communicating skills		I understand how to create a range of opportunities for children to communicate science to a range of audiences	
If you feel that you have any areas of uncertainty in this column then you should turn to the activities in Getting Started on **page 39**.		*If you feel that you have any areas of uncertainty in this column then you should turn to the activities in Developing your Skills on* **page 65**.		*If you feel that you have any areas of uncertainty in this column then you should turn to the activities in Extending your Skills on* **page 91**.	

Chapter 2 Assessment and recording in science

In this section you will consider different aspects of assessment and recording in science. Assessment and recording are part of a cycle that involves planning, teaching, assessing, planning and so on. This cycle is at the heart of teaching.

This section will cover:

➲ questioning;
➲ other strategies for formative assessment.

Assessment is the process of collecting evidence and making judgements about children's achievements. In science the judgements that you make about children's achievements will be mostly concerned with their **ideas** and with how scientific their ideas are. That isn't the whole picture though. You will also make judgements about the children's **skills** in working scientifically (such as their ability to set up a fair test) and the extent to which they have developed scientific **attitudes** (such as curiosity).

Questioning

You can use a range of methods for collecting evidence and making judgements about children's achievements. Some of these methods are outlined below. The most obvious method – and possibly the most important – is the teacher asking questions. Questions can be used to find out about the ideas the children hold and to help them to develop their ideas further. Similarly, they can be used to find out about what level of skills the children already have and to help them consolidate and develop their skills. In the earlier scenario Mrs Martineau had targeted some of her questions to certain children, whom she felt may struggle with the concepts involved in floating and sinking, in order to make sure that she had enough information about the progress that they made.

Wynne Harlen's writing is particularly useful in providing guidance for questioning in science (Harlen, 2000a). She draws helpful distinctions between different types of questions and outlines their potential value. For example:

Open or closed questions
Open questions are especially valuable in science for enabling children to give an account of their own ideas, to share their thinking freely, to hypothesise and predict and to review their thinking. By contrast, closed questions are more useful for probing understanding, for making connections with previously encountered ideas, for checking accuracy and identifying misconceptions.

Subject- or person-centred questions
Subject-centred questions are the typical closed questions that teachers may ask, where a child either knows or doesn't know the right answer. '*Why does the heavy boat float?*' would be an example. These can be intimidating, particularly to those less confident in science, and may result in the child guessing randomly in an attempt to come up with what the teacher is thinking. By contrast, a person-centred question asks children for their own ideas – '*Why do you think the heavy boat floats?*' Children can't get these wrong, so they are more likely to result in the children giving an accurate representation of their ideas.

Productive or unproductive questions
A productive question is one that leads on to further thinking, discussion or enquiry, unlike unproductive ones which tend to close the conversation down. Productive questions promote:

- observation (e.g. 'have you noticed that …?')
- comparison (e.g. 'which of these is …?')
- measurement (e.g. 'how long is …?')
- action (e.g. 'what would happen if …?')
- problem solving (e.g. 'can you find a way to …?')

These questions are useful in other ways apart from assessment. Open and productive questions are especially useful for helping children to pursue their own enquiries and work in a scientific way (see Teaching practical science section, **page 17**). Exploring their value for assessment is a useful way to build them into professional practice.

Other strategies for formative assessment

Some of your assessments in science will be summative assessments at the end of a lesson or a topic. However, most of your assessments in science will be ongoing formative assessments. In some cases they may be based on tangible evidence that you can collect and look at later. This can be useful since it means you can take some time over making judgements about the children's achievements and thinking about whether and how you might need to adjust your planning and teaching. In other cases the evidence is less tangible but still useful, enabling you to adjust your teaching at the time or to rethink your planning and teaching later.

How you go about formative assessment in science is less obvious than in literacy and numeracy, where the kinds of activities that children engage in generally allow you to make a direct judgement about their achievements (e.g. can they construct sentences using full stops and capital letters, or can they count on in 5s?). What you will want to avoid is spending a lot of time in assessing children instead of helping them to learn. Ideally you want to find ways of assessing that are also useful teaching/learning activities.

Fortunately there are quite a lot of assessment methods that you can use in science that can also be valuable teaching/learning activities. Here are some examples.

- Asking questions and listening to children's responses. Open questions and person-centred questions can be especially useful – see Harlen (2000a; 2000b) for further guidance.
- Listening carefully to the words that children use when they talk about science.
- Structured drawing, including annotating drawings, sequencing drawings and completing pictures.
- Structured writing, including sequencing statements, completing a table and producing a report.
- Free writing and drawing, such as individual diary or group log book.
- Concept maps, which offer a structured way to enable children to represent their ideas – see Harlen (2000a; 2000b), Sharp *et al.* (2002) or White and Gunstone (1992) for further guidance.
- Grouping, sorting and classifying activities.
- Matching activities, such as matching words and definitions.
- Structured activities such as True/False statements.
- Concept cartoons, which invite children to discuss the science involved in an everyday situation – see Naylor and Keogh (2000) for further guidance.
- Children's self-assessment, which means that they need to be aware of what the goals are for their learning.

In the earlier scenario Mrs Martineau had used the children's responses to a concept cartoon and their group presentations as a means of informal assessment. This had enabled her to feel confident that most of them had developed a good understanding of some other factors that are important, and that some were confident about how forces are involved in floating and sinking. Her assessments had been built in as a natural part of her teaching, so the children hadn't noticed that any assessment was taking place.

These assessment methods are highly suitable for finding out and making judgements about the children's scientific ideas. Some of them can also provide useful information for assessing their scientific skills. However, scientific skills are part of a dynamic process, and there is often not much tangible evidence that children have engaged successfully in that process. Observing them during scientific enquiries, talking to them about their enquiries and looking at how they record their enquiries are likely to be the most useful things you can do to assess their skills. Interacting with the children as they investigate is the ideal approach but this may not always be possible. This is one of the reasons why teachers often find it quite difficult to assess children's scientific skills.

Think about Mrs Martineau's lesson. What opportunities did she have for assessing scientific skills:

- ⊃ during the lesson?
- ⊃ when working with the small group?
- ⊃ at the end of the lesson?
- ⊃ in the maths lesson next day?

The evidence used to make summative judgements often comes from an accumulation of the formative assessment judgements made over a period of time. Teachers can use their professional judgement to come to an overall view about individual children's progress. Alternatively it is possible to use specific tasks or tests that enable the children to demonstrate their achievements in a particular aspect of science. Frequently teachers will use a combination of these two approaches.

In addition to the summary judgements that teachers make there are also National Tests set by QCA, the Qualifications and Curriculum Authority. The National Tests for science set at the end of Key Stage 2 are an example of statutory assessment against the National Curriculum level descriptions. Teachers are involved in preparing children for these tests but are not involved in either setting or marking them. Although in principle these National Tests can provide useful information to teachers, they do have the unfortunate consequence of many teachers teaching to the test and sacrificing children's learning in an attempt to gain higher test scores.

Assessing your needs

How far have you developed your understanding of assessment and recording in science? Reflect on the needs assessment grid below and if possible discuss your ideas with a colleague, teacher or tutor.

Needs assessment: assessment and recording in science

Getting started	Date	Developing your skills	Date	Extending your skills	Date
I have observed teachers using questioning with children learning science		I am aware of a range of strategies for formative assessment in science		I have ensured that my assessment and recording in science is in line with the school's policy	
When planning to teach science to a group of children I have thought about the kind of questions that I can ask		I have used and evaluated a range of formative assessment strategies in my science teaching		I understand how to plan for and use diagnostic, formative and summative assessment in science	
I have used questions to explore scientific ideas with different age groups of children		I have made a record of the outcomes of formative assessments		I understand how to make effective records of children's progress and report their attainment in science	
When teaching a group of children I have tried to evaluate the questions that I have used		I have found out about a school's science assessment policy and used it to inform my practice		I understand how to use local and national data for science to inform my planning	
*If you feel that you have any areas of uncertainty in this column then you should turn to the activities in Getting Started on **page 39**.*		*If you feel that you have any areas of uncertainty in this column then you should turn to the activities in Developing your Skills on **page 65**.*		*If you feel that you have any areas of uncertainty in this column then you should turn to the activities in Extending your Skills on **page 91**.*	

In their drive to manage what goes on in schools and to raise standards of achievement in external assessment, successive governments have made a series of changes to the system in England and Wales. They have taken control over what is taught, introducing a National Curriculum, National Strategies and Schemes of Work. Increasingly they are directing how teachers teach, with, for example, the National Literacy Strategy laying down very detailed guidelines for classroom organisation, timing and sequences of activities. However, it is clear that these measures have not achieved, and will not in themselves achieve, the objectives that governments have had in mind. As any trainee teacher soon discovers, suitable lesson content and classroom organisation are necessary but not sufficient conditions for success in the classroom.

One of the major factors that is often ignored is the importance of how children feel about being on the receiving end of what teachers offer. Whether or not children are motivated to learn is crucial. As Woolnough puts it, '*If students are motivated, and if they are given the freedom and opportunity, they will find ways of learning. If they are not, they will not bother*' (1994: 111).

Child motivation is influenced by a number of factors. These include:

➲ the context for the activity and whether it appears to have any purpose or meaning;
➲ the context for the subject and whether it seems relevant or connected in any way with children's real-life experiences;
➲ the nature of the subject and the views that children have of whether they are capable in that subject;
➲ children's roles in the classroom and the relationships they have with the teacher and with other children.

Clearly these factors suggest that certain kinds of teaching approaches will be more successful at motivating children than others. Fortunately science as a subject tends to be inherently interesting to primary age children. In many schools this is evident in their reluctance to go out to play when the lesson ends, in their enthusiastic attendance at science clubs, and in their ongoing interest in science outside school. So, in a way, teachers start with an inbuilt advantage when they are teaching science. Children will sometimes be motivated in science in spite of poor teaching, whereas with good teaching motivation is almost guaranteed.

One of the elements of good teaching is that it promotes inclusion – in other words, it provides suitable learning opportunities for all children, regardless of their background or individual learning needs. The National Curriculum sets out three principles for developing an inclusive curriculum (DfEE, 1999):

➲ setting suitable learning challenges;
➲ responding to children's diverse learning needs;
➲ overcoming potential barriers to learning.

These are demanding principles for any teacher. In science they have a number of practical applications. For example:

➲ **Practical investigation** is an important feature of many science lessons. Although it is difficult to generalise, research shows that boys frequently tend to monopolise equipment and to dominate in 'hands-on' activities, with girls often taking on the role of recording results. Simply providing the opportunity for practical investigation may not be sufficient. An inclusive approach might require the teacher to manage access to resources and children's roles during the activity in order to overcome this potential barrier to learning.

⮞ **Assessment** is another area where careful thought is needed to promote an inclusive approach. Research indicates that girls and boys often respond differently when being assessed. On the whole, short, structured assessment items (such as multiple-choice questions) tend to favour boys, while questions requiring more extended writing tend to favour girls. Similarly, any assessment that relies on children completing work at home will tend to favour those children with supportive home environments and parents who are interested in their child's education.

⮞ The **images of science** presented to children carry very strong messages about whom the subject is for. What do the images appear to say about the social and cultural background of people who are scientists? What do they suggest that scientists do when they are working? What do they indicate about whether science is an isolated or a collaborative activity? It is not necessary to portray scientists as the caricature 'mad professor' for children to get the feeling that science is for other people and not for them. Fortunately publishers have made much progress recently in producing materials with images representing people from a wide range of social and cultural backgrounds.

⮞ The **language** used in science has a very important influence on inclusion. Too much technical vocabulary, use of the passive voice ('the salt was placed in the water') instead of the active voice ('we put the salt in the water') and complex sentence structures make reading about science an impossible task for some children, especially those with English as an additional language. The balance between providing access for all and using language as a means of providing challenge is not an easy one to get right. However, science does provide a wealth of opportunities for communicating in a variety of ways, including diagrams, tables, charts, models and computer-based communication, and children who struggle with one form of communication may be more fluent with another.

Reiss (1998) gives further examples of some of the practical implications of inclusion in science, and Ratcliffe and Lock (1998) offer some guidance on learning about the social and ethical applications of science.

These examples begin to illustrate how science can help to contribute to children's spiritual, moral, social and cultural development, as required by the National Curriculum. Science provides opportunities for children to reflect on their place in the world; to base judgements on evidence rather than preconceptions; to develop a different understanding of social issues; and to recognise some of the important links between science and culture. The range of types of activities that children engage in while they are doing science makes it an invaluable subject for addressing these aspects of learning.

Another area in which science makes a vital contribution is that of thinking skills. Thinking requires a purpose, and scientific enquiry provides this. Scientific enquiry is all about searching for fundamental patterns of how the world works. Thinking skills are seen in children who can find out instead of having to be told; who don't just notice what happens but begin to think about why it happens; who can solve problems without waiting for someone else to give them the solution. The movement to promote thinking skills in schools has gained ground in recent years, with quite a few schools viewing this as central to their curriculum. Unfortunately the National Curriculum only pays lip service to them, and the strong emphasis on subject knowledge in the National Curriculum and Standard Tests tends to give the impression that they are not important.

In order to promote thinking skills it is important for teachers to provide cognitive challenges that give children something to think about; to provide meaningful contexts that are likely to engage their attention; to offer opportunities for collaborative working, since much of what children know is socially constructed knowledge; and to get children to review and reflect on their learning so that they build up suitable habits of mind. Writings by authors such as Fisher (1990) provide useful guidance for developing thinking skills across the curriculum.

In the scenario described earlier, Mrs Martineau may not have had all of these factors in mind when she planned her lesson, but it is evident that she has a good grasp of how they are important and views thinking skills as integral to science. She starts her lesson with a meaningful context to motivate the children and engage their attention. She values their ideas and builds on these in the investigation. She sets suitable challenges that are adjusted to recognise the children's individual learning needs. She provides an environment in which collaborative working (independent of the teachers) is expected and roles are negotiated and monitored. She sets cognitive challenges and helps the children to review and reflect on their learning. As a role model she's not bad!

Assessing your needs

How far have you developed your understanding of other aspects of science education? Reflect on the needs assessment grid below and if possible discuss your ideas with a colleague, teacher or tutor.

Needs assessment: other aspects of science education

Getting started	Date	Developing your skills	Date	Extending your skills	Date
I have observed teachers to see how they motivate children in science		I have reviewed the school policy and resources in terms of inclusion		I have identified issues to explore in my practice	
I have found out what kinds of images of and attitudes to science many of the children have		I have reviewed the school policy and resources in terms of thinking skills		I have used an action research approach to explore issues	
I have thought about how to promote inclusion and motivation in my planning		I have reviewed my planning and teaching in terms of inclusion		I have implemented an action research approach in my teaching	
I have thought about the school policy in terms of inclusion		I have reviewed my planning and teaching in terms of thinking skills		I subject my teaching to ongoing review and evaluation	
*If you feel that you have any areas of uncertainty in this column then you should turn to the activities in Getting Started on **page 39**.*		*If you feel that you have any areas of uncertainty in this column then you should turn to the activities in Developing your Skills on **page 65**.*		*If you feel that you have any areas of uncertainty in this column then you should turn to the activities in Extending your Skills on **page 91**.*	

Guidance and Needs Analysis ⇒
Conclusion

There is much to learn about teaching within science and across the primary curriculum as a whole. It is easy for your work in school to become random and reactive so that there is no structure to your experiences or direction to your learning. Trainees often find it difficult to know where to start and to identify what the important next steps are for their learning. Now that you have completed the needs analysis section for each theme, you should be able to use these to negotiate a plan with your class teacher or mentor to give a clear focus to your work in your school or class.

The grid on page 38 gives an overview of all the activities for each stage of development. You could highlight the areas that you need to cover to use in your initial planning and discussions to gain an overview of your learning needs and how they can be addressed. You will find more detailed grids for each stage at the beginning of the next three chapters. These will help you to form a detailed individual training plan (ITP) to support and direct your work in school. If you are also using other Learning Matters workbooks, or other material to guide your learning, you should consider how the ITPs for each subject might be used together to structure your whole experience in the school.

It is important that you involve other people in the needs analysis process. The following people will be helpful in different ways:

⇒ your course tutor;
⇒ your school tutor/mentor;
⇒ your class teacher/mentor;
⇒ other trainees.

In some schools you may find that you will negotiate your training plan with the head teacher *prior* to the start of the placement to ensure that the school is in a position to provide the best experience possible.

You should also involve some of the people above in assessing how much progress you are making and whether there is the need to amend your ITP in the light of this assessment.

Guidance and needs analysis: overview of ITP

Theme	Getting started	Developing your skills	Extending your skills
1 Progression in ideas	Finding out about children's ideas and how they develop • Observe children in different age groups • Talk to children in different age groups • Consider the development of children's ideas • Look at progression in the school and/or QCA Scheme of Work	Exploring children's ideas to help plan effectively • Explore own understanding • Look at progression in the Scheme of Work in relation to the topics taught • Research children's misconceptions • Begin medium-term planning • Assess children for progression in ideas	Learning how to respond to children's misconceptions • Research likely misconceptions • Plan intervention strategies • Try out and evaluate intervention strategies • Make targeted observations in other classes to support aspects of personal learning
2 Teaching and learning strategies	Learning about how teachers teach science • Observe science teaching and children's responses in different age groups • Try out and evaluate different strategies	Learning about models and analogies • Identify resources for modelling concepts • Identify resources for children's independent research • Plan to use models, analogies, etc. • Use and evaluate models, analogies, etc.	Learning about strategies for teaching science • Extend and justify the range of strategies used • Use a greater range of strategies and evaluate these • Make targeted observations in other classes to support aspects of personal learning
3 Teaching practical science	Planning to help a small group of children observe effectively • Observe practical work in science in different age groups • Plan to develop observation skills • Teach a small group practical • Observe science investigation	Learning about teaching practical science • Observe children fair testing • Plan whole class teaching of practical activities • Teach practical science lessons	Teaching children to engage in critical thinking • Plan for progression in investigative skills • Teach investigative skills and evaluate strategies • Look for evidence of successful learning • Make targeted observations in other classes to support aspects of personal learning
4 Classroom management, organisation and resources	Finding out how teachers manage their class when teaching science • Observe aspects of classroom management in different age groups • Consider the implications of different management strategies	Exploring effective management of science with the whole class • Observe strategies used for practical work and other kinds of enquiry • Plan practical and research-based lessons • Use and evaluate strategies • Check details in the school safety policy and ASE guidelines	Look at aspects of management in your teaching • Review aspects of management • Become more aware of how other teachers manage science • Look for any impact of selected approaches • Evaluate selected management strategy • Make targeted observations in other classrooms to support aspects of personal learning
5 Planning and teaching science	Planning for a small group science activity • Look at and evaluate other teachers' plans • Plan for small group activity • Evaluate your own planning	Planning for whole class teaching • Planning to include sense of purpose • Planning to include questions • Find out how teachers approach differentiation in science • Differentiation and assessment in planning • Planning a sequence of lessons • Evaluate planning and teaching	Extending your planning skills • Identify levels of planning • Make planning more effective • Amend planning • Link planning and evaluating • Evaluate selected aspects of planning • Make targeted observations in other classrooms to support aspects of personal learning
6 Children communicating and recording science	Learning about how children can communicate their ideas in science • Listen to how children use scientific terminology • Look for examples of how children record and communicate in science • Plan recording strategies for a group • Evaluate recording strategies	Learning about ways of recording science • Look for examples of children recording results and using ICT • Select a range of methods to record results with a class; plan to use ICT • Evaluate different recording methods; evaluate use of ICT	Looking at communicating science through literacy and numeracy • Plan for links with literacy • Plan for links with numeracy • Incorporate aspects of literacy and numeracy into science teaching • Make targeted observations in other classrooms to support aspects of personal learning
7 Assessment and recording in science	Learning how to question in science • Observe how teachers use questioning • Plan to use different styles of questioning with a group • Use different styles of questioning • Evaluate different styles of questioning	Learning about assessment • Find out about the school's assessment policy • Review a range of formative assessment methods • Try out a range of formative assessment methods • Evaluate formative assessment methods	Using summative formative assessment in science • Plan for and use formative assessment • Review school policy on summative assessment • Make formative and summative judgements • Plan for recording children's achievement, record and report children's progress • Make targeted observations in other classrooms to support aspects of personal learning
8 Other aspects of science education	Learning about motivation and inclusion as an important part of science teaching • Find out about children's images of science • Notice how teachers motivate children • Look for inclusion and positive images in the policy for science • Identify opportunities to promote inclusion and motivation in planning	Taking account of inclusion and thinking skills • Talk to the science co-ordinator and review policy and resources for inclusion • Review planning and teaching in terms of inclusion • Talk to the science co-ordinator and review policy and resources for thinking skills • Review planning and teaching in terms of thinking skills	Carrying out classroom-based research to consider inclusion and/or thinking skills • Explore specific issues in practice • Implement action research approach • Make targeted observations in other classrooms to support aspects of personal learning

Contents

Introduction	39
Progression in ideas	41
Teaching and learning strategies	43
Teaching practical science	46
Classroom management, organisation and resources	49
Planning and teaching science	51
Children communicating and recording science	54
Assessment and recording in science	57
Other aspects of science education	60
Conclusion	63

Introduction and individual training plan

The activities in this section are for trainee teachers who have had very limited experience of teaching science. You may have spent some time in a classroom but you will have little awareness of what teachers do when they are teaching science or the basic ideas about how children learn science.

In the grid on page 40 we have identified the activities that you will be carrying out for each theme. Most of the activities are to be carried out in a school setting, although preparation might be carried out elsewhere. There are spaces in the grid so that you can identify the activities that you will cover and agree with the school when and where you will carry them out. This will be your individual training plan (ITP) for the Getting Started stage of your development. You may not need to do all of the activities if you have had some experience in school already. If time is short you will need to prioritise the activities. You should be able to carry out the activities in this chapter over a six- to eight-week period, providing that you have at least one lesson a week in your base class and access to other classes in the school.

You will need to make decisions about the order in which you carry out the activities. If you have very limited experience we would recommend that you spend some time at the start of your placement observing science teaching with different ages. Each theme includes observation activities, some of which can be linked together. When going into another class it is essential that you negotiate with the teacher what you will be observing and the parameters of what you can or cannot record or discuss later. Observation of other colleagues teaching requires a high level of professional trust and respect.

Most activities also involve planning and teaching science to a small group of children. Each activity has a different emphasis to help you to learn about the different aspects of teaching science. Theme 5 (**page 51**) takes you through the process of planning. You may wish to do the activities in that theme first before engaging in the activities in the other themes.

Theme	Page ref	Activities	Links to other activities	Links to QTS Standards	When and where the activity will be carried out
1 Progression in ideas	p. 41	Finding out about children's ideas and how they develop • Observe children in different age groups • Talk to children in different age groups • Consider the development of children's ideas • Look at progression in the school and/or QCA Scheme of Work	You could carry out some small group observation tasks together, e.g. talking to children about their ideas and how they communicate (theme 6)	2.1b; 2.3; 3.1.1	
2 Teaching and learning strategies	p. 43	Learning about how teachers teach science • Observe science teaching and children's responses in different age groups • Try out and evaluate different strategies	You could carry out some whole class observations together, e.g. how teachers teach science and how they question (theme 7)	2.7; 3.1.1; 3.1.2; 3.3.3; 3.3.6	
3 Teaching practical science	p. 46	Planning to help a small group of children to observe effectively • Observe practical work in science in different age groups • Plan to develop observation skills • Teach a small group practical • Observe science investigation	You could carry out planning activities together, e.g. planning practical work and learning about planning (theme 5)	3.3.1; 3.3.2; 3.3.3	
4 Classroom management, organisation and resources	p. 49	Finding out how teachers manage their class when teaching science • Observe aspects of classroom management in different age groups • Consider the implications of different management strategies	You could carry out some whole class observations together, e.g. how teachers manage teaching and how they question (theme 7)	3.1.1; 3.1.3; 3.3.7; 3.3.8	
5 Planning and teaching science	p. 51	Planning for a small group science activity • Look at and evaluate other teachers' plans • Plan for small group activity • Evaluate your own planning	You could carry out planning activities together, e.g. learning about planning and planning practical work (theme 3)	1.7; 3.1.1; 3.1.2	
6 Children communicating and recording science	p. 54	Learning about how children can communicate their ideas in science • Listen to how children use scientific terminology • Look for examples of how children record and communicate in science • Plan recording strategies for a group • Evaluate recording strategies	You could carry out some small group observation tasks together, e.g. how they communicate and listening to their ideas (theme 1)	1.7; 3.2.1; 3.3.5	
7 Assessment and recording in science	p. 57	Learning how to question in science • Observe how teachers use questioning • Plan to use different styles of questioning with a group • Use different styles of questioning • Evaluate different styles of questioning	You could carry out some whole class observations together, e.g. how they question and how they motivate children (theme 8)	1.7; 3.2.1; 3.2.2	
8 Other aspects of science education	p. 60	Learning about motivation and inclusion as an important part of science teaching • Find out about children's images of science • Look for how teachers motivate children • Look for inclusion and positive images in the policy for science • Identify opportunities to promote inclusion and motivation in planning	You could carry out some small group observation tasks together, e.g. finding out their ideas about science and how they communicate (theme 6)	1.1; 1.2; 1.3; 1.7; 3.3.1; 3.3.3; 3.3.4; 3.3.5; 3.3.6; 3.3.14	

Chapter 3   Progression in ideas

Link to Professional Standards for QTS

The activities in this section address the following Standards for the award of QTS:

2.1b; 2.3; 3.1.1.

Introduction

Working towards progression in the children's knowledge and understanding of scientific ideas is a challenging aspect of science teaching. This section is designed to help you to begin to recognise some of the important aspects of progression, including:

- ➲ how an individual child's scientific ideas might develop;
- ➲ how scientific ideas might develop over long periods of time, and how this leads to a range of ideas in a class;
- ➲ how a school Scheme of Work might support you in your teaching.

There are three activities within in this theme. The first two activities involve talking to children about their ideas and listening to their discussions. You need to be aware that children do not always have the vocabulary to describe their ideas fully at an early stage. You need to also remember that progression is more complex than simply knowing scientific ideas.

Preparation
Read the introduction to Progression in children's ideas in Chapter 2 and pay particular attention to the table on **page 10**. Arrange to observe children being taught science.

Discuss with the class teacher the ideas that are being developed and look in the National Curriculum, the Foundation Stage Document or the QCA Scheme of Work to see if the children might have covered this concept before. Try to identify the ideas and misconceptions they might hold.

Task
Ideally you need to create the opportunity to observe a class being taught a topic in science over a number of lessons or to spend time in the class at the beginning and the end of a topic. Listen to the children's responses to the teacher and to each other. Selecting a small number (say 3 or 4) of children to focus on may make this easier.

Evaluation and follow up
What do you notice about the children's ideas at the start of the topic?
Do they have any ideas that surprise you?
What do you think about their overall level of understanding at the start of the topic?
Can you see any evidence of progression and development in their ideas by the end of the topic?
Are you able to describe the nature of progression in their ideas? For example:

- ➲ from concrete to more abstract ideas?
- ➲ from specific to more general ideas?
- ➲ from ideas that apply in a single context to ideas that apply more widely?
- ➲ from vague to more precise ideas?

Your observations and reflections should help you to become more aware of what you are aiming for in planning for progression.

Preparation
Choose a topic that you feel fairly familiar with and prepare some questions which you can use to elicit children's ideas. You may find *Nuffield Primary Science* (1993) or Johnsey *et al.* (2002) are helpful in doing this.

Task
Talk to some children in different age groups about their ideas in this topic. You may well find it easier to talk to a small group out of the classroom (e.g. at playtime).

Evaluation and follow up
➲ What range of ideas do the children have?
➲ How well do their ideas fit with National Curriculum expectations?
➲ Can you see evidence of how effective teaching has been in helping to develop the children's ideas in this topic?
➲ To what extent do their early confusions and misconceptions seem to be retained as they get older?
➲ What do you think the implications of the children's ideas might be for your teaching if you were to teach this topic?

Thinking about these questions will help you to become more aware of how your teaching needs to take the children's ideas into account.

Preparation
Obtain a copy of the school's science documents including the school Scheme of Work for science, or the QCA Scheme of Work.

Task
Think about the topic you addressed above. Look for how progression in children's ideas is described or how progression is planned for in the school. There may be a general section that describes progression or it may be discussed in several parts of the document.

As you read you should consider:

➲ How does it describe the nature of progression in children's ideas?
➲ How does it give support to teachers to help children's ideas to progress?
➲ Does it give any indication of some of the difficulties in teaching so as to promote progression?
Now take a topic such as plants and identify progression in the learning objectives for the topic in the various age groups in which it is taught.

Evaluation and follow up
It will be useful to discuss your initial ideas about progression in this topic with the class teacher(s) or science coordinator if you have the opportunity.

➲ How does the class teacher think that the children's ideas will progress?
➲ What indicators does s/he look for as evidence of progression?
➲ What are the class teacher's views about the implications for teaching of the expected progression in ideas?

Thinking about these questions will help you to understand better what progression can mean in planning for teaching.

Johnsey, R, Peacock, G, Sharp, J and Wright, D (2002) *Primary science: knowledge and understanding* (2nd Edition). Exeter: Learning Matters.
Various authors (1993) *Nuffield Primary Science Teachers' Guides*. London: Collins Educational.

Your achievements

Now that you have completed these activities you should be able to:

➲ identify the development of children's ideas within the teaching of a topic;
➲ talk to children about their ideas and recognise progression across several age groups;
➲ identify progression in a Scheme of Work.

Link to Professional Standards for QTS

The activities in this section address the following Standards for the award of QTS:

2.7; 3.1.1; 3.1.2; 3.3.3; 3.3.6.

Introduction

In this theme you will spend some time observing science teaching with a focus on the teaching and learning strategies being used. You will already have your own preconceptions of what you are likely to see. These may well be based on your own experience as a learner of science in school. In order to develop your understanding you will need to consider these preconceptions alongside what you observe. It is likely that you will see a variety of practices. You may find a mismatch between what you expect to see and what happens in reality. At times the teaching you see may confirm your ideas but you should still think carefully about the effect on children's learning of the strategies being used. It is important that, wherever you can, you talk to the teacher about what you have observed.

There are two activities in this theme, one involving observation of teaching and the other planning and teaching science to a small group of children.

Preparation

Read through the introduction to different teaching and learning strategies as outlined in Chapter 2. You also need to negotiate to observe science teaching in several classes of children, preferably from different Key Stages. You need to ensure that you are aware of the strategies that you might observe. The grid below summarises some of those that have been previously discussed. You also need to be aware of the kinds of observations and judgements that you are going to make. These are across the top of the grid. You should show the grid to the teacher prior to the observation to ensure that it is seen as acceptable or to see if the teacher wishes to modify it.

Task

While you are observing the teachers look for the strategies that they are employing. How do the children respond to different approaches? Do they all respond in the same way? Use the grid below to identify which teaching strategies were used and in which context (e.g. demonstration of the effect of heat on some materials, whole class investigation of mirrors, small group practical measuring growth). You may find it helpful to discuss the grid with each teacher before the lesson to identify which strategies you are likely to observe. If you use the same grid for each observation make sure that you use a different coloured pen or a different code to identify each class. Remember that every strategy has advantages and disadvantages and varies in its effectiveness for children's learning.

Read Mrs Martineau's story in Chapter 2 (**page 6**).

Observing teacher strategy

The teacher: ／ The children:	are motivated and attentive	show interest and attention some of the time	show little interest or attention in the science
tells/gives/explains information (exposition)			
demonstrates a practical experiment (e.g. cooking or burning)			
uses whole class practical investigations			
uses small group activities			
caters for individual children with special needs			
encourages children's own research using ICT, books, families, etc.			
uses analogies and 3D models to explain scientific ideas			
trains children in the safe use of science/ maths equipment			
arranges a school visit or visitor			
provides stimulating introductions			
conducts thoughtful plenaries			
presents a good role model: curious, enthusiastic and open-minded			

Evaluation and follow up

Are there any strategies that seem to always motivate the children? Are there some that are consistently less helpful in motivating children to learn? Are there differences between the ways that different children respond? What does this tell you about their preferred learning styles? How does this relate to your own experiences of learning in science?

Discuss the children's responses with the teacher or your mentor.

Background

As you may now have seen, the choice of teaching strategy can be significant in motivating children to learn. Part of that motivation stems from the attitudes shown by the teacher towards science and the children, and how the children perceive themselves:

- ➲ as receivers of the teacher's knowledge;
- ➲ as participants in the journey of discovering and learning;
- ➲ as valued equally with every other member of the class;
- ➲ as co-operating detectives looking for and evaluating evidence;
- ➲ as sharing with the teacher feelings of curiosity, enthusiasm, critical reflection.

In this activity you will have the opportunity to use the teaching strategies of: introducing a science session, small group activity and demonstration

Preparation

Arrange to teach two or more groups in the class to which you are attached. If this is a new class spend a little preparation time getting to know the children in the selected group (find out their names, ages, interests) and what the teacher can tell you about their skills and knowledge of science. Ask the teacher about their special needs and/or precautions that may be necessary. You can carry out an activity that the teacher had already planned or plan something yourself. You may be able to work with two groups during one afternoon. Alternatively you may need to negotiate carrying out this activity over two sessions.

Task

Teach science to two small groups of children:

⮕ with you demonstrating the activity to one group; and
⮕ with the other group engaged in a small group practical activity.

Think about using different stimulating introductions to the science sessions. Use a different introduction for each group (e.g. a story, showing the objects, asking for predictions, etc.).

Use the grid below to evaluate the effectiveness of the strategies. Note down the type of introduction you used and the nature of the practical/demonstration.

Evaluating different strategies

	Introduction	Demonstration	Small group practical
Did this capture and retain the children's attention?			
How effective was this in encouraging: Scientific skills? Observation? Other general skills?			
Did this strategy enable you to speak to each child and offer positive feedback?			
Did this strategy enable you to listen to each of the children and hear their ideas?			
Did this strategy give you the opportunity to show yourself as an interested learner alongside the children?			

Evaluation and follow up

Discuss the sessions afterwards with the class teacher. Did your introductions stimulate the children's attention? How did the children respond to the demonstration compared with the responses to the small group practical? Did the two teaching strategies stimulate and encourage the children's scientific skills and ideas?

Goldsworthy, A and Holmes, M (1999) *Teach it! Do it! Let's get to it!* Hatfield: ASE.
Harlen, W (2000) *The teaching of science in primary schools* (3rd Edition). London: David Fulton, Chapters 7 and 9.

Your achievements

Now you have carried out these activities you should be able to:

⮕ introduce science to a small group of children;
⮕ plan and carry out a small group science activity;
⮕ demonstrate a simple scientific idea to children;
⮕ recognise different teaching and learning strategies.

Link to Professional Standards for QTS

The activities in this section address the following Standards for the award of QTS:

3.3.1; 3.3.2; 3.3.3.

Introduction

Setting and achieving learning objectives in practical science might appear to be quite tricky when you are just getting started. The key to success is to focus on one scientific skill at a time. Other learning will undoubtedly take place but focusing on one objective allows you to plan appropriate resources, select relevant and challenging questions and recognise evidence of learning when children employ this skill. Even when you have become confident in targeting science knowledge objectives, it is normally advisable to target one scientific skill, or small group of related skills, in each science session. To develop in this area you will do three activities, involving the observation of teaching, planning and teaching a practical science activity with a small group of children and observing science investigation.

Background

The skill of observing is chosen for the following activities as this skill permeates all good science from childhood to scientific research. Primary children can often give the impression that they 'don't need to look' as they 'know' what's there. So it is important for teachers to target this skill repeatedly, with reminders and encouragement to observe carefully each year, from Reception to Year 6.

Observing includes the senses and mathematical observing (estimating, measuring, weighing, etc.). Children's progress in skilful observing is shown in their increasing sophistication in the use of mathematical tools (e.g. tape measures, callipers, capacity jugs) and the confident use of sense-enhancing equipment (e.g. hand lenses, microscopes, thermometers, digital balances, digital/computer light and heat sensors).

Preparation

Arrange to observe children carrying out practical science activities. If possible observe children in different age groups and/or different Key Stages. Note that it is not always safe or appropriate for children to use *all* their senses in a practical activity.

Create a grid like the one below for each group observed to note down what you see the children observing.

Observing practical science	
What did the children:	**What was the focus of their observation?**
Notice (see)?	
Hear?	
Feel?	
Smell?	
Taste?	
Measure using standard units?	
Measure using non-standard units?	

Task

Either work with a group of children or observe the children from a distance. Choose which feels most appropriate for the class that you are working with at the time.

Complete the grid as you observe the children.

Evaluation and follow up

Discuss what you noticed with a colleague. Did the children notice features of objects or what was happening? Were the children measuring? Did they use different senses? Did the teacher have to do anything special to ensure that the children used their senses? Are some activities or ways of working more appropriate for helping children to develop the skill of observing? Can you see any difference between observation as used by a 5-year-old and by an 11-year-old?

Preparation

Discuss the current science focus with your class teacher.

Collect five or six different objects related to the focus for the children to observe, such as:

- ➲ plants/growth – a bunch of flowers, a set of different fruits or seeds;
- ➲ forces – balls, wind-up toys;
- ➲ sound – musical instruments;
- ➲ electricity – a set of different electric light bulbs.

Make sure you have a variety of objects and decide in advance whether you will cut things open or take them apart and the extent to which the children can explore the objects safely (in other words, carry out a risk assessment for how safe the activity is). Try to include at least one item that is unfamiliar to the children.

Look at the school resources for science and maths that will encourage and enhance observing and measuring, including ICT tools. Decide whether you will need measuring tools (e.g. measures, balances) and/or observation equipment (e.g. hand lenses). Collect the necessary resources for this and for drawing the objects (drawing will focus their observing skills).

Identify a small group of children to carry out the science activity. Prepare a grid similar to the one above to note down what your children noticed about the objects.

Task

Set out the objects but explain to the children that they are not allowed to touch the objects for five minutes (they can use other senses).

Ask each child to tell you what they notice. Some children will notice the same thing as others, which is perfectly acceptable – you can encourage their attention by approving their first comment and asking, *'Do you notice anything else?'* If necessary, guide the children's attention to particular features, using questions such as *'Do you notice anything the same about the objects?'*

When you think it is appropriate, encourage the children to explore and/or measure the objects in other ways, communicating what they notice. Finish by asking the children to make careful, detailed drawings. You might want to help children who are less confident by joining in the drawing (do not worry if you do not feel good at drawing – it is the recording of observations that is important).

Evaluation and follow up

Complete the grid in the previous activity to capture your observations of the children. You can do recordings for individual children if this is helpful.

Use your notes to discuss with the class teacher the effectiveness of your small group practical activity in encouraging children's skilful observation. Talk about the strategies that seemed to help the children to observe. Did you try any of the strategies that you have seen used elsewhere? How effective were they?

Background

Scientific enquiry includes scientific investigation as well as finding out in other ways. The current version of the National Curriculum makes it clear that the use of secondary sources is part of genuine scientific enquiry. Fair testing is the most common and most important type of scientific investigation that the children will carry out. However they don't simply discover how to investigate on their own; they have to be taught how to do this.

Preparation

Read the sections in the National Curriculum for science on scientific enquiry (pages 78, 83–4). Read about the nature of scientific investigation in any recent text, such as Harlen (2000) chapter 9 or Sharp *et al.* (2002) chapter 3.

Task

Find some opportunities to observe some science teaching, preferably in more than one age range. Check with the teacher before the lesson whether s/he will be doing any scientific investigation with the children.

When you observe any science teaching in school you should look for key points.

➲ How do teachers set up scientific investigation with the children? For example, do they always begin with whole class discussion? How does the starter activity lead into the investigation? Do they use a planning frame with the children? Do they use a recording frame? Do all the children do exactly the same activity?

➲ How do the children respond to the opportunity to carry out scientific enquiries? Do they seem involved and motivated? Do all the children respond in a similar way? Do all the children take on similar roles when they are investigating, or do some children always have the same role (e.g. recording results)?

➲ How do scientific enquiries provide opportunities for children's learning? What kinds of skills do they seem to be learning? Are you surprised by any aspects of what the children are able to do or what they do not do?

Evaluation and follow up

Find the appropriate section of the National Curriculum and/or Scheme of Work for the age group you have been observing. Use these to reflect on the science teaching you have observed. What do you feel are the key elements in teaching scientific investigation successfully? What do you think you will need to include in your planning when you teach scientific investigation yourself (with small groups initially)?

---

de Boo, M (1999) *Enquiring children, challenging teaching: investigating primary science.* Buckingham: Open University Press.

Harlen, W (2000) *The teaching of science in primary schools* (3rd Edition). London: David Fulton. Especially Chapters 9 and 10.

Jarvis, T (1995) 'What shall we put in the fruit salad? Developing investigative thinking and skills in children', in J Moyles (ed.) *Beginning teaching, beginning learning*, pp. 115–128. Buckingham: Open University.

Your achievements

Now you have carried out these activities you should be able to:

➲ plan and carry out practical science activities with a small group;
➲ develop children's learning in a scientific skill;
➲ begin to evaluate the effectiveness of using practical science to develop scientific skills;
➲ recognise the key elements in scientific investigation.

Classroom management, organisation and resources

Link to Professional Standards for QTS

The activities in this section address the following Standards for the award of QTS:

3.1.1; 3.1.3; 3.3.7; 3.3.8.

Introduction

In the early stages of becoming a teacher you will need to develop your awareness of the issues that influence classroom organisation for science, both through your background reading and through observation of teaching. In doing this you will reflect on the effectiveness of the different organisational strategies used in science lessons and begin to make decisions about which strategies you might employ in your own teaching. There is one main activity that you will carry out at this level that focuses on observing science teaching and two follow-up activities to evaluate what you have observed. You should read the whole section before you start so that you know what you are to observe.

Preparation

In order to carry out the activity you should read the introductory section in Chapter 2 (**page 19**) about classroom organisation and management. You may also find it helpful to read Sharp *et al.* (2002) Chapter 7. You also need access to a copy of *Be Safe* (ASE, 2001).

Negotiate access to at least one class in Key Stage 1 and one in Key Stage 2. If possible talk to the teacher before the lesson so that you are aware of the strategies that might be used. This will avoid your spending time trying to guess what decisions the teacher has made.

Copy the grids like the one below to help you to reflect on your observations. You can use the grids when discussing the lesson with teachers.

Task

Spend some time observing how the classes are organised and managed in terms of:

➲ the organisation of practical activity (e.g. teacher demonstration, whole class activity, small group activity, individuals);
➲ groupings used for science (e.g. literacy ability groups, numeracy ability groups, mixed ability groups, friendship groups);
➲ organisation of and access to resources (e.g. teacher distributes resources, monitor system to distribute resources, independent access).

These are listed in some detail in the grid on page 50.

Observing classroom organisation and management

Organisation	Whole class demonstration	Large groups	Small groups	Pairs	Individuals
Children responded positively and kept on task					
Children talked about their scientific ideas					
Children required a lot of support					
Children were able to work well on their own					
Grouping	**Maths groups**	**Literacy groups**	**Same ideas groups**	**Mixed ideas groups**	**Friendship groups**
Children responded positively and kept on task					
Children talked about their scientific ideas					
Children required a lot of support					
Children were able to work well on their own					
Access to resources	**Teacher sets out the resources**	**Monitor system**	**Resources are available in a central area**	**Children can access their own resources with permission**	**Children can access their own resources**
Children responded positively and kept on task					
Children talked about their scientific ideas					
Children required a lot of support					
Children were able to work well on their own					

Evaluation and follow up 1

Reflect on the different types of grouping and organisation that you observed. Use the grid above to help you reflect on what your experience has shown you. Use different colours to show the different age groups. How do the different aspects of the organisation of each lesson compare in terms of successful classroom management? Do you see any differences between age groups? Do younger children require different management styles?

Discuss your findings about classroom organisation with a teacher, mentor, tutor or colleague. Highlight which successful strategies you would like to try in your own teaching and which strategies need high levels of management skills or need to be modified to enable you to use them.

Evaluation and follow up 2

Look at the relevant section(s) of *Be Safe* (ASE, 2001). What specific guidance is relevant to the lessons that you have observed? Can you see how and when the teacher(s) took this guidance into account?

ASE (2001) *Be safe* (3rd Edition). Hatfield: ASE.
Sharp, J, Peacock, G, Johnsey, R, Simon, S and Smith, R (2002) *Achieving QTS. Primary science: teaching theory and practice* (2nd Edition). Exeter: Learning Matters. Chapter 7.
Waterson, A (2000) 'Managing the classroom for learning', in K.Jacques and R.Hyland (eds.) *Achieving QTS. Professional studies: primary phase*, pp. 74–92. Exeter: Learning Matters.

Your achievements

Now you have carried out these activities you should be able to:

➲ understand different organisational strategies for science;
➲ identify different groupings for science;
➲ identify different strategies for managing resources.

Chapter 3   Planning and teaching science

Link to Professional Standards for QTS

The activities in this section address the following Standards for the award of QTS:

1.7; 3.1.1; 3.1.2.

Introduction

If you are carrying out the activities in this section then it is likely that you have not planned for science before. By the end of your first period of time in school you should aim to have covered all aspects of planning similar to that identified in Chapter 2. Trainee teachers often make the mistake of not putting sufficient detail in their early planning and therefore often fail to anticipate problems or issues that might arise. It is essential that you have mentally walked through your plan, trying to anticipate when problems might arise, how resources might be used, how learning might be optimised and to visualise what you and the children are going to do and think about. For example, you cannot run round the school looking for practical resources once the lesson has begun or create support material for a child needing additional help within the lesson.

There are two main activities in this section. The first invites you to evaluate a plan for science. The second begins to look at your own planning for science and what needs to be involved.

Preparation
Look at the section on planning in Chapter 2, **page 22**. Look very carefully at Mrs Martineau's plan on **page 25**. If you can gain access to the daily planning of your teacher or other teachers, have a look at the key elements that they regularly include. You are likely to find some variation in the plans, as there is no single definitive planning format.

Task
Look at Gavin's plan on **page 52** and compare it to Mrs Martineau's plan and other plans that you have seen.

- How much support would Gavin's plan give you if you had to teach his class?
- What might the children learn from the lesson?
- Does this plan match his learning objectives?
- What are the strengths of his plan? What needs to be developed?

Write down what you would want to tell Gavin about how his planning might be improved.

LESSON PLAN			
Subject: science		**NC ref:** change of state	
Date: 5 March	**Duration:** 1.75 hrs	**Class:** Year 2	**Number of children:** 24

Children's prior learning
The teacher did some work on change last week

Key vocabulary Change, melt, solid, liquid, heat, cool, boil, freeze, harden	**Learning objectives** • Understand how to carry out an investigation • Understand how to record an investigation • Learn that things change when they are heated – some are reversible

Lesson sequence

Intro Talk to the children on the mat about what changes when it is heated, – e.g. chocolate, ice, egg Show children the worksheet to be filled in. Check that Emmie and Patrice know what they are doing	**Group activity** Children work through the sheet and tick things that they think will change Let children try things out using warm water or night lights (groups with teachers) I will work with red group and Mrs Bradshaw with green group	**Discussion** What did they find out?
Differentiation By outcome	**Assessment** Look at their worksheets to see if they are filled in	**Resources** Substances, night lights, sand trays, tongs, warm water in flask, spoons, beakers, worksheets

Safety
No problems – I will be with the group with the night lights

Gavin's plan

Evaluation and follow up
Discuss your evaluation of Gavin's plan with your teacher or mentor to make sure that you are developing insight into what should be included in an effective plan.

Preparation
Look at the National Curriculum and a unit of work from the QCA Scheme of Work for science or the teacher's medium-term planning. With the help of your class teacher decide what area of science you can teach to a small group. This could be part of a lesson that the teacher would otherwise plan.

Task
Using the headings from Mrs Martineau's plans, construct a plan for your teaching. Make sure you start by identifying the learning objectives before you decide on the teaching activity. Complete the rest of the planning and try out your planning by teaching the lesson to a small group.

This first attempt at planning could be linked with one or more of the other activities in this chapter, e.g. theme 3.

Evaluation and follow up
After you have taught the group, evaluate your planning with the aid of your teacher or mentor and write an evaluation of your plan. You can use the following questions to help to structure the discussion.

- ⮐ How well did the plan support your teaching?
- ⮐ How much thinking did you need to do on the spot?
- ⮐ How much did you need to clarify once the children had started to work on their own or in groups?
- ⮐ How well did you use the conclusion of the lesson to help the children to reflect on their own learning?
- ⮐ To what extent did the activities allow the learning objectives to be met?
- ⮐ In what ways does your planning need to develop for the next time you are teaching science?

Naylor, S and Keogh, B (1998) 'Differentiation', in R. Sherrington (ed.) *ASE guide to primary science education*, pp. 140–7. Hatfield: ASE.

Sharp, J, Peacock, G, Johnsey, R, Simon, S and Smith, R (2002) *Achieving QTS. Primary science: teaching theory and practice.* Exeter: Learning Matters, Chapter 6.

Your achievements

Now that you have completed these activities you should be able to:

➲ evaluate planning;
➲ plan and evaluate lessons for groups of children.

Chapter 3 Children communicating and recording science

Link to Professional Standards for QTS

The activities in this section address the following Standards for the award of QTS:

1.7; 3.2.1; 3.3.5.

Introduction

When planning you should always consider the key vocabulary that you would wish the children to understand as Gavin did in his plan on **page 52**. The QCA Scheme of Work includes information about vocabulary at the front of each Unit. Teachers find this helpful when deciding what vocabulary they wish to develop and how they might use language to extend and challenge the scientific understanding of some children. It also enables them to prepare resources that will help other children to use key scientific vocabulary more effectively.

In this section you will look at two aspects of children's communication in science: using scientific vocabulary and recording science.

Preparation
Using the QCA Scheme of Work for science, find out what vocabulary children are expected to use for different units of work. Choose a topic area and identify the progression in vocabulary from Key Stage 1 through lower and upper Key Stage 2. The grid below has been completed by looking at all the units that involve electricity as an example. You will need to make a grid like the one below to record your findings.

Using scientific vocabulary		
Key Stage	**Year/Unit**	**Vocabulary**
Key Stage 1	Year 2/F	Bulb, bulb holders, buzzer, battery, switch, circuit, connection, mains, wire, break, brighter, less bright
Key Stage 2 (early)	Year 4/F	Battery, bulb, buzzer, motor, break, electrical conductor, electrical insulator, metal, plastic
Key Stage 2 (later)	Year 6/F	Complete circuit, conductor, insulator, circuit symbol, component, circuit diagram, cell

You should be able to see from grid the language that the children should have met at an early stage and that which might be introduced later in their development of conceptual understanding in an area of science. The same activity could be carried out for the development of the language associated with procedural understanding (Sc 1).

Task
If possible arrange to spend some time with a small group of children from different age ranges (such as Year 2, Year 4 and Year 6). Ideally you need to talk to them briefly about the area of science you have looked at in your grid. If this is not possible you could offer to support teachers while the children are doing science and focus on the areas that they are teaching. It is not necessary for you to have planned a lesson, as the focus of your work is listening to the vocabulary that the children use in science.

Ask the children about their understanding of specific terminology. Can they explain what the words mean and not just use them?

Make notes of the scientific vocabulary that they use. How does this match with the expectations in the QCA document?

Evaluation and follow up
Are you surprised by the vocabulary that children are expected to use? Did any children surprise you by the vocabulary that they used?

While you are with children learning science be alert to the way that teachers introduce new scientific words to the children. Do all teachers use the correct terminology all the time? How do they ensure that the children understand what they are saying? Maybe they use the specific vocabulary alongside an everyday explanation – for example, *'friction: how much grip something has'*. Talk to teachers about how they help children to learn new terminology.

Preparation
Here is a list of ways that children might record and communicate their ideas and results in science. Recording does not always have to be written in exercise books.

- Filling in a recording framework.
- Producing a scientific report.
- Completing a table, Venn diagram, graph or chart.
- Answering a set of questions.
- Writing a letter.
- Producing a report for a newspaper/magazine/radio show.
- Producing a set of instructions.
- Producing an information leaflet.
- Creating a poster.
- Creating a display.
- Contributing to a group or class display.
- Drama presentation.
- Creating an advertisement.
- Drawing a picture.
- Labelling a picture.
- Sequencing text and/or pictures.
- Producing a sequence of text and/or pictures.
- Writing a poem.
- Writing a story.
- Making a book.
- Contributing to a group or class book.

All of these may be independent or with support – from peers, from an adult, from a structured framework or from explicit guidance. Consider which of these might be completed independently by a 5-year-old child and which might be completed independently by a 9-year-old child. Which of the above have you used for recording science as a learner?

Task 1
When you are walking round the school be alert to the ways that science is recorded and communicated. Ask permission to look in children's science books and talk to teachers, particularly the science co-ordinator, about strategies that are used in the school. Keep a record of these ideas and add them to your list.

Task 2
When you plan a science activity for groups of children pay particular attention to how and why they are going to record their results. If possible try some different methods of recording from the list above. Make sure the children are aware of the fact that their results are going to be communicated to others since this will help to give them a sense of purpose.

Task 3
Find an opportunity to talk to the children about how and why they record science. Who do they think it is for? Do they think that it communicates their ideas to anyone else? Can they make suggestions of effective ways of communicating science to peers, teachers, parents and the whole school?

Evaluation and follow up
Reflect on what you have learnt about recording in science. Can you make any judgement about which strategies for recording and communicating were most effective? You may be able to create a checklist to use as an *aide-mémoire* for your future planning.

Burton, N (1995) *How to be brilliant at recording in science.* Leamington Spa: Brilliant Publications.
Feasey, R (1998) *Primary science and literacy.* Hatfield: ASE. Topics 3 and 4 deal specifically with scientific vocabulary.
Harlen, W (2000a) *The teaching of science in primary schools* (3rd Edition). London: David Fulton, Chapter 12.

Your achievements

Now that you have completed these activities you should be able to:

➲ understand how children's scientific vocabulary develops;
➲ have some ideas for how to introduce scientific vocabulary;
➲ support children in using a range of strategies for recording scientific enquiry.

Chapter 3   Assessment and recording in science

Link to Professional Standards for QTS

The activities in this section address the following Standards for the award of QTS:

1.7; 3.2.1; 3.2.2.

Introduction

Getting started on assessment in science doesn't have to be complicated or difficult. Think of it as doing what you would be doing anyway when you are teaching science, but in addition being sensitive to what you can find out about the children's ideas and progress. In this section you will be thinking about the questions that you might ask children to find out about their ideas. The focus is on the nature of the questions and the kind of response they provoke, rather than the specific answers that the children give you. First, you will observe teachers to understand the kind of questions that they ask and then you will use your own questions with children.

Preparation
Refer to the section on questioning in Chapter 2 (**page 31**) to remind yourself about the types of questions that teachers might ask in science and how these can be useful for assessment purposes.

Copy the grid below to help structure your thinking about types of questions and to review the way that the children respond to questioning.

Task
Try to find an opportunity to discuss with other teachers how they use questions with children to find out their ideas. This will help you to find examples of the types of questions above. Ideally you should focus on questioning when you observe another teacher during a science lesson and then discuss afterwards how questions were used as part of the approach to assessment in science. You should initially focus your attention on the four types of questions at the top of the grid. As you become more used to listening to questions, you will notice that the question may also be divided into the types shown in the lower section of the grid.

Identifying types of questions

Type of question	Examples	Children's responses
Person-centred		
Subject-centred		
Open		
Closed		
Attention focusing (e.g. What do you notice about … ?)		
Comparison (e.g. What are the similarities between … ?)		
Measuring (e.g. How far did it go?)		
Action (e.g. What do you think will happen if … ?)		
Problem solving (e.g. Can you find a way to …?)		

Evaluation and follow up

Reflect on what you have learnt about how teachers use questions for assessment. What types of questions do the teachers tend to ask most frequently? Which questions seem especially valuable? Don't worry if they do not fit neatly into the categories above.

Preparation

It is assumed that you have already taught science to a group of children and are beginning to get a sense of what this involves. During your teaching you are likely to have used questions but not in any systematic way to assess learning. When you are planning to teach science prepare some sample questions (not a script) that you could use during and at the end of the lesson to assess children's learning. Think about how your questions relate to the learning objective for the lesson. You should keep your questioning fairly simple and try to use both person-centred and subject-centred questions and open and closed questions so that you can see the difference in the responses from the children.

Task

Teach science to a group or groups of children. Use the questions you prepared previously to assess their understanding of the ideas that you have been teaching. These may be ideas about concepts or ideas about procedures.

Discuss the children's ideas with the class teacher if you have the opportunity to do this.

Evaluation and follow up

Create a record like the one below for the children in your groups. At the end of the lesson reflect on what you have learnt about the children's ideas through your questioning and try to decide how well the children have achieved the learning objectives that you set. Ideally you should do this in discussion with your teacher or discuss the record after it is complete.

In the narrow column you should indicate whether you think the learning objective has been achieved. You can do this in many ways. The simplest is ticking and crossing but schools may use something that is a little more sophisticated to show when an objective has been partially achieved. For example, red dot for *not achieved*, yellow dot for *partially achieved* and green dot for *fully achieved*.

The broader column is to add additional information about the exceptional – those children who have struggled, those who found the work too easy or anything significant that a child may have said or done.

Recording assessment						
Children's names	Learning objective		Learning objective		Learning objective	

Review the questions that you used to find out the children's ideas. How valuable were your questions for helping you to make judgements about their ideas? Which of your questions were most useful? Which were least useful? How did your questions compare with the questions that other teachers ask? Can you see ways in which your questioning could be improved?

Feasey, R (1998) 'Effective questioning in science', in R. Sherrington (ed.) *ASE guide to primary science education*, pp.156–67. Hatfield: ASE.
Harlen, W (1905) *Primary science: taking the plunge*. London: Heinemann.
Harlen, W (2000a) *The teaching of science in primary schools* (3rd Edition). London: David Fulton; Chapter 8 and pp.142–3 deal with questioning.
Harlen, W (2000b) *Teaching, learning and assessing science 5–12*. London: Paul Chapman; Chapter 9 deals with questioning.

Your achievements

Now you have carried out these activities you should be able to:

➲ recognise a range of different questions that teachers ask;
➲ plan your own questions;
➲ evaluate how children respond to your questions;
➲ record your assessment of children.

Link to Professional Standards for QTS

The activities in this section address the following Standards for the award of QTS:

1.1; 1.2; 1.3; 1.7; 3.3.1; 3.3.3; 3.3.4; 3.3.5; 3.3.6; 3.3.14.

Introduction

Before starting to work with children it is important to be aware of your own views, images and preconceptions about science. Some useful self-review questions are:

- ➲ What images does science conjure up for you?
- ➲ How does it relate to your everyday life, if at all?
- ➲ What do you see as the benefits and limitations of science?
- ➲ What kind of mental picture is created when you think of someone doing science?
- ➲ How do you feel about learning science?
- ➲ How do you feel about teaching science?
- ➲ What kind of picture of science do you want to help children to create?

Questions such as these will help you to become more aware of your own views, images and preconceptions about science and to identify any perceptions that may need to be challenged. Equally, children may have views that need to be challenged. Stereotyped views can develop in very young children. It is important that schools provide an inclusive learning environment so that all children feel valued and included.

In this section you will carry out three related activities and then reflect on the outcomes of these activities as a whole. In the first activity you will talk to children about their images of science; in the second you will observe how teachers motivate children in science lessons; in the third activity you will look at the images portrayed in written resources and how these materials might support schools in inclusion and motivation. Finally, you will review your planning and teaching against what you have learnt about issues in science education.

Background
Here is a typical picture of a scientist drawn by an 11-year old child. Do children really believe that this is what scientists are like?

Preparation

Think about questions that you can ask children in order to gain their views about science, such as:

- What is special about science as a subject?
- What kinds of people do science?
- Do you see yourself as a scientist?
- Do you do science on your own or together?
- What use is science in your everyday life?

Add to this list as you feel appropriate.

Task

Organise an opportunity to talk informally to children about their views of science. This does not need to take a long time, nor does it need to be carried out in a science lesson.

Evaluation and follow up

Do children carry the stereotypical view of science or are their views more sophisticated than that? Do they have any views that you feel need challenging? How might you challenge these views in your teaching? How might your own perceptions of science influence the children that you teach?

Preparation

Remind yourself of the importance of motivation by reading the relevant section of Chapter 2 (**page 34**).

Task

When you are observing teachers teaching science, focus some of your observation time on what they seem to do to motivate children in science.

Watch the children carefully to see how they respond and try to identify what seems to motivate them.

Evaluation and follow up

If you can, talk to the teachers about how they were attempting to motivate the children. If you can, talk to the children about what they feel motivates them in science.

Afterwards, review what you have learnt about motivating children in science. What have you found out that you can build into your own practice?

Background

The school's science policy and guidelines can be very influential in how teachers address key issues within science education. Some schools have now modified their science documentation to take account of issues to do with inclusion and motivation. This may not be the case in all schools. Other written resources, such as Schemes of Work and child materials, can explicitly and implicitly convey images of science that may or may not be appropriate in promoting an inclusive view of science and enhancing motivation.

Preparation

Make a list of the main issues that you might look for in written documentation for science, such as inclusion, positive images of science, positive images of people from different cultures engaging in science, positive images of gender and science, learning styles, thinking skills, creativity, etc. Talk to the science co-ordinator about whether and how any of these issues have been addressed in school documentation.

Task

Obtain a copy of the school's policy and/or guidelines for science if the head teacher or co-ordinator feels that this will be useful. Alternatively, look at other resources for science in the school, such as National Curriculum materials, the QCA Scheme of Work for science and other published Schemes of Work and related child material.

Evaluation and follow up

What references can you find to inclusion and to promoting positive images? Are any specific strategies suggested for inclusion or for promoting positive images? Does any material convey negative images?

What references can you find to motivating children in science? Are any specific strategies suggested for motivating children in science? Does any of the material appear to be more motivating for children?

Preparation

This activity will be carried out at the end of your time in school. You need to gather together your planning for science, any resources that you may have used or produced and notes made when looking at issues during the previous three activities.

Task

Look at the planning that you have done for teaching science, including any resources you have used.

Building on what you have learnt from talking to children, from observing teachers and from reading the school's policy for science and any other documentation, can you identify any new opportunities in your planning for:

- ➲ motivating children in science;
- ➲ inclusion (that is, providing suitable learning opportunities for all children) in science;
- ➲ promoting positive images in science?

Although your review may not lead to any change in the content of your lessons, it may well lead to some changes in the contexts for learning that you choose and for the teaching and learning styles that you plan to use.

Evaluation and follow up

By now you should be more aware of your own feelings about attitude towards, and perceptions of, science. You should also be more aware of the children's feelings and perceptions. You should also be aware of how these images are reinforced or challenged through written materials available in school.

What actions can you take in your next school placement to ensure that you are more effective at conveying a positive inclusive image of science and an approach and contexts that children find motivating?

Depending on your own prior experience, you may find that you need to do more background reading in this area.

NACCCE (1999) *All our Futures: creativity, culture and education* (the Robinson Report). London: DfEE.
Reiss, M (1998) 'Science for all', in R. Sherrington (ed.) *ASE guide to primary science education*, pp. 34–43. Hatfield: ASE.

Your achievements

Now you have carried out these activities you should be able to:

- ➲ consider issues related to inclusion in your teaching of science;
- ➲ consider issues related to motivation in your teaching of science;
- ➲ review documentation for positive and negative images and attitudes;
- ➲ review your planning and teaching to ensure that more attention is paid to inclusion and motivation.

An important part of professional development is review and action planning. Now that you have completed the Getting Started phase of your development as a teacher you should review what actions you need to take before moving on to the next phase.

For the activities that you have completed in this chapter, you can use the grid below to summarise your professional development. We recommend that you complete this grid in discussion with your teacher, tutor or other professional colleague. In preparation for the discussion tick the activities that you have completed. Rate your confidence level roughly from low to high. Through discussion you have to decide on the actions you need to take to develop your understanding.

The activities in the next chapter are intended to provide the next level of professional challenge. If you are feeling reasonably confident in any of the areas covered these activities should be at an appropriate level to provide progression in your learning. However it is important to think about what additional preparation you could do such as reading, attending courses, assessing and developing your own understanding in areas of science that you have not yet taught.

If you are feeling less confident then using some of the strategies above will be essential to ensure that you are able to make appropriate progress. Part of your development may be to work in school to try out some of the activities again in a new context or to engage in further observation of teaching.

Before leaving this chapter you should ensure that you have started to complete the profiling required by your training provider and that you have acquired that appropriate evidence of your achievement of the Standards.

Getting Started – review and action planning grid

Theme	Activities	Confidence Low → High			Action
1 Progression in ideas	• Finding out about children's ideas and how they develop				
2 Teaching and learning strategies	• Learning about how teachers teach science				
3 Teaching practical science	• Observing teaching and planning to teach a small group of children how to observe effectively				
4 Classroom management and resourcing	• Finding out how teachers manage their class when teaching science				
5 Planning and teaching science	• Planning for a small group activity				
6 Children communicating science	• Learning about how children can communicate their ideas				
7 Assessment and recording	• Learning how to question in science				
8 Other aspects of of science education	• Learning about motivation and inclusion				

Chapter 4   **Developing your Skills** ⇨
Introduction

Contents

Introduction	65
Progression in ideas	67
Teaching and learning strategies	70
Teaching practical science	72
Classroom management, organisation and resources	75
Planning and teaching science	78
Children communicating and recording science	82
Assessment and recording in science	85
Other aspects of science education	88
Conclusion	90

Introduction and individual training plan

The activities in this section are for trainee teachers who have some experience of teaching science. Much of your experience might involve working with groups rather than the whole class, and you may have had little experience of planning on your own.

In the grid on page 66 we have identified the activities that you will be carrying out for each theme. You will see from the grid that it might be possible to link different activities together. Most of the activities are to be carried out in a school setting, although preparation may be done elsewhere. There are spaces in the grid so that you can map out the activities that you will cover and agree with the school when and where you will carry them out. This will be your individual training plan (ITP) for the Developing your Skills stage. You may not need to do all of the activities if you have had some experience in school already. If time is short, you will need to prioritise the activities. You should be able to carry out the activities in this chapter over a six- to eight-week period providing you have at least one lesson a week in your base class and some access to other teachers in the school.

At this point in your professional development you will find that effective planning is a vital part of successful teaching. Themes 1 and 5 look in detail at the planning process. It is essential that you work through the activities in these themes if your experience of planning is limited. You could tackle these themes first before you move on to other sections in this chapter. Alternatively you may have the opportunity to work with your class for a while to get to know the children and to explore different teaching strategies before you begin any systematic medium-term planning. If this is the case it could be more useful to tackle some of the other activities first, including theme 1, before you move on to theme 5.

Some of the activities involve observing other teachers' practice. It is essential that you negotiate with the teachers what you will be observing and the parameters of what you can or cannot record or discuss later. Observation of other colleagues teaching requires a high level of professional trust and respect.

Theme	Page ref	Activities	Links to other activities	Links to QTS Standards	When and where the activity will be carried out
1 Progression in ideas	p. 67	Exploring children's possible ideas to help to plan effectively • Explore own understanding • Look at progression in the Scheme of Work in relation to the topics taught • Research children's misconceptions • Begin medium-term plan • Assess children to look for progression in their ideas	Can be used as preparation for planning (theme 5)	1.7; 2.1; 2.3; 3.1.1; 3.1.2	
2 Teaching and learning strategies	p. 70	Learning about models and analogies • Identify resources for modelling science concepts • Identify resources for children's independent research • Plan to use models, analogies, etc. • Use and evaluate models, analogies, etc.	Can be used as preparation for planning (theme 5)	1.7; 3.1.1; 3.1.2; 3.3.3	
3 Teaching practical science	p. 72	Learning about teaching practical science • Observe children fair testing • Plan whole class teaching of practical activities • Teach practical science lessons	You could carry out this activity at the same time as those in theme 4	1.7; 3.1.1; 3.1.2	
4 Classroom management, organisation and resources	p. 75	Exploring effective management of science with the whole class • Observe strategies used for practical work and other kinds of enquiry • Plan practical and research-based lessons • Use and evaluate strategies • Check details in the school safety policy and ASE guidelines	You could carry out this activity at the same time as those in theme 3	1.7; 2.7; 3.1.3; 3.3.1; 3.3.3; 3.3.7; 3.3.8; 3.3.9	
5 Planning and teaching science	p. 78	Planning for whole class teaching • Planning to include sense of purpose • Planning to include questions • Include differentiation and assessment in planning • Find out how teachers approach differentiation in science • Planning a sequence of lessons • Evaluate planning and teaching	This activity is cross-referenced to the other themes as they all can contribute to effective planning	1.7; 3.1.1; 3.1.2; 3.1.3; 3.1.4; 3.2.1; 3.3.1; 3.3.3; 3.3.4; 3.3.6; 3.3.7; 3.3.8	
6 Children communicating and recording science	p. 82	Learning about ways of recording science • Look for examples of children recording results and using ICT • Select a range of methods to record results with a class; plan to use ICT • Evaluate different recording methods; evaluate use of ICT	Can be used as preparation for planning (theme 5)	1.7; 2.5; 3.1.2; 3.1.3; 3.3.10	
7 Assessment and recording in science	p. 85	Learning about assessment • Find out about the school's assessment policy • Review a range of formative assessment methods • Select and evaluate formative assessment methods	Can be used as preparation for planning (theme 5)	1.7; 3.1.2; 3.2.1; 3.2.2; 3.2.3	
8 Other aspects of science education	p. 88	Taking account of inclusion and thinking skills • Talk to the science co-ordinator and review policy and resources for inclusion • Review planning and teaching in terms of inclusion • Talk to the science co-ordinator and review policy and resources for promoting thinking skills • Review planning and teaching in terms of promoting thinking skills	Can be used as preparation for planning (theme 5)	1.1; 1.2; 1.3; 1.7; 2.4; 3.1.2; 3.3.1; 3.3.1; 3.3.3; 3.3.5; 3.3.6; 3.3.14	

Chapter 4   **Progression in ideas**

Link to Professional Standards for QTS

The activities in this section address the following Standards for the award of QTS:

1.7; 2.1; 2.3; 3.1.1; 3.1.2.

Introduction

By now you will know that children typically bring their own ideas to science lessons and that these existing ideas can make a big difference to how they learn and develop new understanding. Generally there is some rational basis for the children's ideas. They are likely to be related to some kind of experience, although the experience may be limited, it may be gained in a restricted context and the interpretation of the experience may not be accurate.

It is important for teachers to attempt to be aware of the children's existing ideas, and this has implications for how science teaching is organised. For example, knowing what the children's ideas are will help the teacher to be more able to take their ideas into account. So trying to find out, through reading and experience, what the children's ideas might be, and creating frequent opportunities for children to share their ideas within lessons, can help you to make your teaching more effective. It also means that a degree of flexibility in planning is helpful so that it is possible to respond when you find out what ideas the children hold during a lesson.

Feeling confident in your own subject knowledge will help you to be more aware of children's misconceptions. Being aware of your own previous misconceptions can also help you to see how children's ideas might be helped to progress towards a more scientifically accurate view.

In this section there are four related activities. They follow a sequence that should eventually form a normal part of your preparation for teaching science. By dividing the activities up into component parts it may give the impression that planning for science is a long and complicated process. However, you will find that with experience these activities become merged. You will also identify the materials that you find the most supportive in identifying possible progression, likely misconceptions and ways of challenging ideas. The sequence of activities is:

- ⮎ reviewing your own subject knowledge;
- ⮎ identifying children's likely progression in ideas;
- ⮎ identifying likely misconceptions and ways of challenging children's ideas;
- ⮎ planning for science teaching.

Preparation
Discuss with your teacher what areas of science you are going to teach during your time in the school. Obtain some suitable reference material for auditing and developing your subject knowledge and understanding in science (e.g. Sharp and Byrne, 2001; Peacock, 1998).

Task
Use the material to explore your current level of understanding in the topic(s) that you will be teaching. It is important that you are honest with yourself. It is also important that you try to understand the concepts rather than learning a series of facts. When you identify areas of uncertainty or gaps in your understanding you should take whatever steps seem necessary to develop your understanding further – e.g. focused reading, working through relevant problems, discussion with peers and teachers, use of Internet sites, use of video, etc. The best way of carrying out this activity is to talk about the area of science with someone else,

ideally someone else on the same training programme as you. Through talking about your ideas you will be more aware of where your ideas are less secure. If you have any questions they may be answered through Science Line (www.sciencenet.org.uk).

Evaluation and follow up

Think carefully about what has helped you develop your own understanding. Make a note of the key ideas in this area.

Preparation

Gather together the school and/or QCA Scheme of Work for science.

Task

Look at the Scheme of Work for the area of science that you will be teaching. Look at the unit that you will be teaching. Identify the concepts and skills that you will be addressing, paying particular attention to the learning objectives. Look within the unit and at what the children may have covered earlier in relation to these objectives and what they might cover the next time. What guidance does it give you about how children's ideas might progress in the topic? Discuss this with your teacher and/or science coordinator.

Evaluation and follow up

Use this information in the final activity in this section.

Preparation

In order to help children to progress you also need to be aware of the likely misconceptions that they might hold and how these might be addressed. For example, it will help you to be aware of misconceptions such as confusion between melting and dissolving, putting facial features on a shadow, and believing that all heavy things sink in water. You are likely to find that the children hold some of the same misconceptions as you did.

If possible gather together resource material that gives you background about what the children's ideas are likely to be in the lessons that you will be teaching. Examples of suitable resource material include Driver *et al.* (1985), Driver *et al.* (1994), Naylor and Keogh (2000) and Nuffield (1993).

Task

Use this material to make notes about possible activities, questions and teaching and learning approaches that may help to challenge misconceptions and help children's ideas to progress. For example, you may need to think about:

- the range of contexts in which the scientific concept applies;
- a possible range of activities to explore the ideas;
- questions to focus the children's observations more carefully;
- questions to challenge their interpretation of observations;
- how to offer conflicting evidence to challenge their ideas.

Evaluation and follow up

Use your notes in the final activity in this section.

Preparation

You should now be in a position to map out or review the medium-term plan for your teaching in the school. In some situations you may be starting the planning process from scratch. If this is the case then you will need to be systematic in collating the evidence from the ideas and evidence from the three activities above. If your teacher has already prepared such a plan then you should look at the plan and consider how this might be modified in the light of your findings.

Task

Planning for science – keep the outcomes of this activity until you are ready to complete the final activity in the Planning and teaching science section of this chapter (**page 80**).

Evaluation and follow up

After you have taught the series of lessons you should return to this section and carry out the following evaluation activity.

By now you will have realised that planning and teaching for progression is not straightforward. Although progression can be built into a curriculum there is no guarantee that the development of children's ideas will follow a similar pattern. You will almost certainly have experienced teaching a well-planned lesson but been disappointed that some of the children's ideas do not appear to have developed as you intended.

Use a range of techniques (see Assessment and recording in science, **page 32**), including questioning and looking at children's science books or portfolios, to find out whether their ideas have progressed as a result of your teaching.

Useful questions for reflection are:

➲ Have their ideas developed as much as you expected?
➲ Have all the children's ideas developed to the same extent?
➲ Have any of the children retained their initial misconceptions or confusion?
➲ What judgements can you make about what helps your teaching to be successful in promoting the development of the children's ideas?
➲ What would the implications for your teaching be if you were to teach this topic again?

Thinking about these questions will help you to target your teaching to promote progression in the children's ideas.

Reflecting on the range of techniques that you have used to challenge and develop the children's ideas will be helpful, making it more likely that your teaching will be successful. You will find it useful to discuss with the class teacher or science coordinator what action to take when the children's ideas don't appear to have developed as you intended, such as noting this on your assessment records so that the next teacher to teach this topic is aware that further development is needed.

Driver, R, Guesne, E, and Tiberghien, A (eds) (1985) *Children's ideas in science*. Milton Keynes: Open University.
Driver, R, Squires, A, Rushworth, P, and Wood-Robinson, V (1994) *Making sense of secondary science*. London: Routledge.
Naylor, S and Keogh, B (2000) *Concept cartoons in science education*. Sandbach: Millgate House.
Peacock, G (1998) *QTS. Science for primary teachers: an audit and self-study guide*. London: Letts.
Sharp, J and Byrne, J (2001) *Achieving QTS. Primary science audit and test*. Exeter: Learning Matters.
Various authors (1993) *Nuffield Primary Science Teachers' Guides*. London: Collins Educational.
Website www.sciencenet.org.uk

Your achievements

Now you have carried out these activities you should be able to:

➲ reflect on your own understanding of a scientific concept and develop areas of uncertainty;
➲ identify possible progression in children's ideas;
➲ identify likely misconceptions and confusions;
➲ plan for progression and evaluate the effectiveness of your teaching.

Chapter 4   Teaching and learning strategies

Link to Professional Standards for QTS

The activities in this section address the following Standards for the award of QTS:

1.7; 3.1.1; 3.1.2; 3.3.3.

Introduction

You should now have experience of different teaching strategies and should be more aware of the strategies you feel comfortable using and their relative effectiveness in differing circumstances. The use of models and drama to illustrate a scientific concept is a valuable strategy to develop. There are some good commercially produced models and pictures but children often respond even more favourably to the teacher's own models which s/he has produced to support understanding. Dramatising a concept has a positive impact on helping children to clarify their ideas and articulate them through speech and body language. Models and drama can act as informal methods of assessment. They also offer opportunities for your class to communicate ideas to other children and to parents and families, in assemblies or when taken home.

This section develops your skills in using models, analogies and illustrations and in encouraging independent research by the children.

Preparation
Read through the Teaching and learning strategies in Chapter 2, **page 13**, particularly the sections on models and analogies and children's independent research.

Task
With permission from the class teacher and/or science co-ordinator, look into the science resources for items that illustrate or model scientific concepts. For example, you might find big pictures of the solar system or parts of a flower, a model of the eye, a cloth torso and parts of the body, a life cycle game, a globe model of the Earth. Think about how you might use these to introduce a science concept or clarify ideas after a science enquiry. Discuss with the teacher and science co-ordinator the possible use of mime, movement and drama when modelling scientific ideas, as well as verbal analogies and metaphors.

Evaluation and follow up
Use the grid below to evaluate the models and any other images you have seen/observed.

Focusing on models, dramas and illustrations					
	3-D models	Illustrative pictures	Analogies and metaphors	Drama	Mime
Examples seen in use					
Examples seen in school resources					

Preparation

Ask your teacher for information about the individual children you will teach – their experiences and personal skills, their strengths and needs. Find out from research publications and other literature what ideas and misconceptions children at this age are likely to have about the science topic under enquiry (you may have done this already in Progression in ideas, above).

Task

Look into the school's secondary resources for science (books, CD-ROMs, website, videos) and identify relevant resources that your children can access and use for research.

Choose a scientific concept relevant to your science plans.

Either make a 3D-model to illustrate the targeted concept (a well-made model can be the start of your own bank of scientific resources), or plan a drama, mime or movement that will illustrate the concept (Asoko and de Boo, 2002, suggests possible ideas).

Use two of your science sessions with the class to learn more about the use of analogies and research. Plan one session in which you will use the model or analogy (e.g. life cycle of the frog). Use the model/analogy/drama to help children's understanding of the scientific concept, possibly as an introduction or as a plenary to a practical investigation. Plan a subsequent session in which the children will have the opportunity for independent research or feedback from this research (e.g. frog habitats or different species of frog around the world). Encourage children to share their research.

Evaluation and follow up

Discuss with your teacher the effectiveness of each strategy in achieving your objectives, using the grid below to reflect on the teaching strategy. Alternatively, you could ask the teacher to use the grid when observing you working with the children to provide focused feedback.

Focusing on encouraging thinking and explaining, independent research and language and communication		
	The model, analogy or drama used	The nature and focus of the children's independent research
The children were motivated and clarified/explained their ideas when …		
The children were motivated but rather confused in their thinking when …		
The children were enthusiastic in pursuing their research when …		
The children behaved responsibly in pursuing their enquiries when …		
The children were less responsible when …		

Asoko, H and de Boo, M (2001) *Analogies and illustrations: representing ideas in primary science.* Hatfield: ASE.
Various authors (1993) *Nuffield Primary Science Teachers' Guides.* London: Collins Educational.

Your achievements

Now you have carried out these activities you should be able to:

➲ encourage children's independent research using secondary sources;
➲ use analogies to develop children's understanding of scientific concepts;
➲ evaluate the effectiveness and appropriate use of teaching strategies.

Chapter 4   Teaching practical science

C4 Practical science

Link to Professional Standards for QTS

The activities in this section address the following Standards for the award of QTS:

1.7; 3.1.1; 3.1.2.

Introduction

By now you will have taught practical science with small groups of children and observed them carrying out investigations. This section starts you thinking about teaching the whole class carrying out science investigations. There are two activities in this section. The first emphasises fair testing as a central feature of scientific investigation. The second focuses on children raising questions and making predictions.

Background

Drawing conclusions from the evidence is only valid if the evidence has been collected in a scientific way – that is, by fair testing. A yellow ball may bounce higher than a black ball but were both balls dropped or was one of them thrown down? Is one ball bigger than the other? Did they both bounce on the same surface? How many tests were carried out? Does the colour of the balls matter?

Fair testing is about controlling the variables (or factors) in an investigation so that reasonable conclusions can be drawn from the evidence. In other words, a number of factors must be kept the same (such as ball size, drop height, surface) and only *one* variable is changed. This is called the independent variable – say, comparing a golf ball with a squash ball. Then the dependent variable (bounce height) is measured several times to get an average test result. It is not expected that young children will use the terminology of dependent and independent variables but they should be developing an understanding of factors affecting an investigation on which later understanding of variables will be based (see 'Scientific Investigation and Enquiry' in the National Curriculum).

In reality, no investigation in primary science can ever be totally controlled or totally fair (a golf ball is heavy, a squash ball is lightweight) but children can begin to understand the principle of fair testing: that unless tests are repeated and done under controlled conditions, no justifiable conclusions can be drawn. Young children have an awareness of what is 'unfair' first ('Robbie pushed *his* car down! It's not fair!'). Teachers' questions that encourage children to think include, '*How can we make it fair for everyone*?' At KS1, teachers will need to control most of the variables in advance. Children progress in their skill of fair testing as they begin to control the variables themselves and decide which features to keep the same, which variable will be changed and which one will be measured and how.

Preparation

Organise an opportunity to observe classes of children carrying out practical science. Tell the teachers that you are focusing on fair testing to check whether their lesson would be appropriate for you to observe. Discuss with them what strategies they are using to include fair testing as a part of their teaching. Copy the grid below to use to support your reflections.

Observing fair testing			
The context of the science practical	The teacher controlled most/all of the variables	The teacher and children planned together	The children controlled most/all of the variables
What were the children comparing?			
What were the children measuring?			
Were the tests reasonably fair?			

Task
Spend some time observing each class. It may be better if you do not join in with the teaching of these activities as you want to have the opportunity to see how much the children can do on their own. However, you need to respond appropriately to each situation as a professional.

Evaluation and follow up
Discuss with the class teachers the strategies they used to encourage children's skills and understanding of fair testing, using the grid to support your discussion.

Background
Earlier in Chapter 2 you were encouraged to think about the teacher's questions. Teachers' questions can challenge children's thinking and support their investigating as well as assess their learning. However, even with excellent teachers' questions, we want to encourage children's own questions. These questions motivate children to pursue their *own* enquiries (not '*ours*'), reveal children's existing ideas and encourage language skills. Not all of their questions will be investigable. Part of the skill that they need to develop is to recognise the difference between those questions that they can investigate and those which can't be investigated in a typical classroom, however fascinating the question!

Teachers often find that after a year or two in school the children seem to stop asking questions. This suggests that we need to give real encouragement to children if they are to ask meaningful questions which promote scientific investigation. Some strategies to encourage their questions are:

- brainstorming with the whole class to get them used to generating questions freely;
- using stimuli to promote questions, such as problems posed to the children;
- collecting questions and saving them for later when they can be considered more carefully;
- enabling children to ask questions anonymously, such as with question boxes or question boards;
- making questions visible, through displays, mobiles, question boards and so on;
- valuing questions so that the children see that their questions can make a real difference to the direction of a lesson;
- evaluating questions so that the children recognise the difference between productive and less productive questions.

Further examples of useful strategies are given in Feasey (1998).

Making predictions
'*I wonder what will happen if ...*' Making predictions starts the children thinking and establishes a focus for their investigations and conclusions. If children have had little experience of predicting prior to a science enquiry, they may lack confidence. One way to increase their confidence is to ask the children – in pairs or threes – to discuss what they think and make a joint prediction. You can also offer your own ideas to show that it is normal for something different to happen from what you expect. Part of learning about science is to think about why the unexpected occurred. Children can be surprised rather than disappointed if their predictions don't come true as long as they do not see predicting as a test. Some children may try to 'manage' the investigation or make inaccurate observations because they have predicted an outcome. Predictive skills progress from the inexperienced personal response to predictions that are based on prior experience and then predictions that are based on emerging theories or hypotheses.

Preparation

Plan a whole class practical science session. Choose an investigation that all the children can carry out simultaneously – e.g. investigating absorbency of different papers, solubility of different materials in water, electrical conductivity of different materials, dropping time of parachutes or numbers of seeds in rose-hips. Then:

⮞ Collect enough resources so that each group has enough to work practically with a degree of independence. Make sure additional resources are easily accessible to reduce unnecessary movement or crowding.

⮞ Decide on your role during the practical.

⮞ Set up a chart or class display to record the children's questions and predictions.

Task

Introduce the whole class to the activity by showing the objects to be investigated. Then:

⮞ Ask the children for as many questions as they can think of, as individuals or in pairs, and write their questions down.

⮞ Ask the children which questions could be investigated, given the resources available.

⮞ Select a question together for the enquiry and ask the children to predict as many possible results as they can think of and write these down. (Writing down children's ideas values both the ideas *and* the children.)

⮞ Decide how you will control the other variables in the investigation – for example, how much water to add, what will count as 'dissolved', how high the drop should be, how many times to test and so on.

⮞ Use the plenary to discuss why the children made their predictions and what the results might mean.

Evaluation and follow up

⮞ Think about how you might use some of the children's questions in further investigations if you have time.

⮞ Reflect on what the children's questions and predictions reveal about their scientific knowledge and their ability to predict.

⮞ Note down any successes or benefits of using a whole class approach in encouraging children's scientific skills.

de Boo, M (1999) *Enquiring children, challenging teaching: investigating primary science*. Buckingham: Open University.

Feasey, R (1998) 'Effective questioning in science', in R Sherrington (ed.) *ASE guide to primary science education*, pp. 156–167. Hatfield: ASE.

Goldsworthy, A and Feasey, R (1997) *Making sense of primary science investigations* (2nd Edition). Hatfield: ASE.

Goldsworthy, A and Holmes, M (1999) *Teach it! Do it! Let's get to it!* Hatfield: ASE.

Harlen, W (2000) *The teaching of science in primary schools* (3rd Edition). London: David Fulton, especially Chapters 13 and 20.

Your achievements

Now that you have carried out these activities you should be able to:

⮞ teach a whole class practical science session;

⮞ encourage the development of children's scientific skills;

⮞ evaluate the effectiveness of whole class teaching for practical science investigations.

Chapter 4 — Classroom management, organisation and resources

Link to Professional Standards for QTS

The activities in this section address the following Standards for the award of QTS:

1.7; 2.7; 3.1.3; 3.3.1; 3.3.3; 3.3.7; 3.3.8; 3.3.9.

Introduction

You now need to organise to teach the whole class for science. You are already aware of different aspects of organisation and management that you need to consider but, so far, it has not been you that has been responsible for putting them into place. The activity in this section will be carried out as part of your planning for science teaching with the whole class. You will teach two lessons and evaluate the effectiveness of your teaching against a range of criteria. The criteria relate to the indicators of good practice that were outlined on **page 8**. You will focus on:

- ease of organisation;
- children's active engagement;
- children's independent working;
- opportunities for scientific investigation;
- opportunities for research;
- opportunities for discussion.

Preparation

If you are in a new school you may want to look at the way that the teachers organise science before you teach the whole class. You are in a new context and different factors may influence decisions about the management of science, such as how independently the children work, whether they are used to working in groups and the children's behaviour. As before, you should consider organisation, grouping and resources – but you should now also consider classroom layout.

You should also use the grid on **page 50** and the evaluation of any experience you have had of teaching science to help you to reflect on classroom organisation. Highlight in the grid which classroom management strategies you feel are likely to be successful for you in your teaching. Consider which aspects you have the skills to manage at this stage. You may wish to plan this lesson jointly with your teacher if you have had little experience of planning for science.

Task

Plan a science lesson that involves the children in practical investigation:

- consider how you will organise the class in terms of activities, sequencing, timing, grouping, use of space and access to resources;
- identify any potential problems with these aspects of classroom management;
- adjust your plans where necessary so as to minimise any potential problems;
- look at the relevant section(s) of *Be Safe* (ASE, 2001);
- identify any potential safety hazards and how these can be avoided.

Plan a lesson that involves the children in researching and finding out information:

- consider how you will organise the class in terms of activities, sequencing, timing, grouping, use of space and access to resources;
- identify any potential problems with these aspects of classroom management;
- adjust your plans where necessary so as to minimise any potential problems;
- look at the relevant section(s) of *Be Safe* (ASE, 2001);
- identify any potential safety hazards and how these can be avoided.

Evaluation and follow up

After each of these lessons reflect on what you have experienced, using the matrix below to organise your thinking. This will help you to identify what supports successful classroom management of science in your teaching. You need to think about your management in terms of the outcomes for the children. There are several aspects that you should consider. These include:

- ⮕ Were the children actively engaged?
- ⮕ Were the arrangements easy to organise?
- ⮕ Did the children work independently?
- ⮕ Were there opportunities for the children to engage in scientific investigation and enquiry?
- ⮕ Were there opportunities for the children to discuss their ideas?

Evaluating aspects of classroom management

My own classroom management	CRITERIA FOR MAKING JUDGEMENTS: ORGANISATION						
	Children actively engaged	Easy to manage	Children work independently	Opportunities for scientific investigation	Opportunities for scientific research	Opportunities for discussing ideas	Other criteria
Successful strategies							
Less successful strategies							
Strategies where success is variable							
My own classroom management	CRITERIA FOR MAKING JUDGEMENTS: GROUPING						
	Children actively engaged	Easy to manage	Children work independently	Opportunities for scientific investigation	Opportunities for scientific research	Opportunities for discussing ideas	Other criteria
Successful strategies							
Less successful strategies							
Strategies where success is variable							
My own classroom management	CRITERIA FOR MAKING JUDGEMENTS: CLASSROOM LAYOUT						
	Children actively engaged	Easy to manage	Children work independently	Opportunities for scientific investigation	Opportunities for scientific research	Opportunities for discussing ideas	Other criteria
Successful strategies							
Less successful strategies							
Strategies where success is variable							
My own classroom management	CRITERIA FOR MAKING JUDGEMENTS: ACCESS TO RESOURCES						
	Children actively engaged	Easy to manage	Children work independently	Opportunities for scientific investigation	Opportunities for scientific research	Opportunities for discussing ideas	Other criteria
Successful strategies							
Less successful strategies							
Strategies where success is variable							

Highlight in the matrix those aspects that were less successful. Before your next science lesson reflect on the following statements in relation to each of these strategies. Share your evaluation with your class teacher or mentor to help you in planning for your teaching.

I think … was a less successful strategy because:

- ➲ I did not have enough experience to use this strategy properly;
- ➲ this strategy is not suitable for the activity that I had planned;
- ➲ this strategy would not work in the way I tried to use it;
- ➲ the children are not used to working in this way;
- ➲ I did not make myself clear to the children;
- ➲ other events outside my control affected the children's response;
- ➲ it was the right strategy on the wrong day;
- ➲ I was trying to do too much at once;
- ➲ I had not thought it through carefully enough in my planning;
- ➲ (… other possible reasons…).

You need to keep these ideas in mind when evaluating your science teaching until you reach a point where you feel confident in the decisions you are making about classroom management and organisation.

Feasey, R (1998) *Primary science equipment.* Hatfield: ASE.

Hollins, M (1998) 'Resources for teaching science', in R. Sherrington (ed.) *ASE guide to primary science education*, pp. 206–15. Hatfield: ASE.

SCIcentre (1999) *Primary science classroom organisation* (video). Leicester: University of Leicester and University of Cambridge.

Sharp, J, Peacock, G, Johnsey, R, Simon, S and Smith, R (2002) *Achieving QTS. Primary science: teaching theory and practice.* Exeter: Learning Matters, Chapter 7.

Your achievements

Now that you have carried out these activities you should be able to:

- ➲ organise a lesson for teaching science;
- ➲ consider the classroom layout for science;
- ➲ think about access to resources.

Chapter 4   Planning and teaching science

Link to Professional Standards for QTS

The activities in this section address the following Standards for the award of QTS:

1.7; 3.1.1; 3.1.2; 3.1.3; 3.1.4; 3.2.1; 3.3.1; 3.3.3; 3.3.4; 3.3.6; 3.3.7, 3.3.8.

Introduction

This section is aimed at developing your skills of planning. Ideally you will draw on activities carried out in other sections – for example, progression in children's ideas, classroom management, organisation and resources – in order to complete this section. However it is likely that you will need to plan at the start of your time at school. If so you should plan your first lesson then use other activities to review and develop your planning. Aspects of planning are considered separately, but as you develop more experience you will be able to think about planning more holistically. However, it is important that your future planning incorporates the elements included in this section.

You will carry out four activities. These focus on creating a sense of purpose for the children, using questioning, building in differentiation and planning a series of lessons in science.

Background

Children need to see a clear sense of purpose in their activities if they are to fully engage in the learning process. Activities in some schemes or other guidance material may be well matched to the National Curriculum requirements but may not be well matched to the children's interests.

Preparation

Have a copy available of the medium-term planning for your class and any initial short-term planning that you have done (see Progression in ideas, **pages 67–69**).

Task

Below is a grid with some learning objectives and activities completed. The teacher has been trying to ensure that all her activities have a clear sense of purpose for the children rather than being a routine that they will follow. Some of the information has not yet been completed. Can you fill in the blanks in the grid to identify activities with a clear sense of purpose?

Matching activities to learning objectives and giving them a sense of purpose		
Children should learn:	**Planned activity with no clear sense of purpose**	**Planned activity with a clear sense of purpose**
that water is transported through the stem to other parts of the plant	Children draw and label a picture from a book showing how water is transported through the stem	
that food chains begin with a plant	Children make up food chains using a set of cut-out cards	
that some materials are more waterproof then others	Children drop water on pieces of fabric	
that shiny objects need a light to shine	Shining a torch on different objects in a dark place to see if they reflect light	
that solids can be separated from liquids by filtering	Practise using filter paper	Making real coffee from coffee beans

Evaluation and follow up

Now put some of your own learning objectives in the left-hand column of the grid. If you have already planned some activities, where will you put them? Will they go in the sense of purpose column? If not, how can you change them so that they do have a clear sense of purpose for the children?

Background

You should now be aware of the importance of questions in science. If you completed the activities in Chapter 3, Assessment and recording in science (**pages 57–59**), you will have already considered questioning in relation to how it helps you to become aware of the children's ideas and to respond to them.

Preparation

Use the grid below to help you to think about different types of questions that you might use when you are investigating insects or melting and dissolving. Some examples have been completed for you.

Include questions in your planning	Grasshoppers		Dissolving	
Type of question	Person-centred	Subject-centred	Open	Closed
Attention-focusing	What do you notice about the grasshopper's legs?	Does it have spikes on its legs?	What can you see happening to the sugar?	Has all the sugar dissolved?
Comparison				
Measuring				
Action				
Problem solving				

Task

Now carry out the same process to create a list of questions that you can ask the children during your lessons. Consider whether your questions are suitable for children with different levels of achievement and how you might be able to adjust your questions to make them more accessible or more challenging.

Evaluation and follow up

Think about the questions that you asked the children. Did the answers require the children to think? Was the level of questioning appropriate for the age range and the attainment of individual children? If you were observed, what comments did the teacher/mentor/tutor make? Write a list of ways in which you may be able to improve your questioning skills.

Background

Differentiation in science often feels quite different from differentiation in English or mathematics. Although differentiation by task is sometimes used, it is more common to use other strategies for differentiation in science. The close matching of activities to children's learning needs is problematic in science for a number of reasons: you won't have detailed knowledge of the children's capabilities, the learning demand of science activities is difficult to define, and matching capabilities and demands is very tricky.

Preparation

Naylor and Keogh (1998) list a number of strategies that can be useful for promoting differentiation in science, including:

➲ using a range of learning styles, so that the teaching and learning approach is more likely to be suitable for all the children;

➲ targeting support for some individuals or groups, such as additional language support, extra-vigilant monitoring or simply spending more time with them;

◗ varying the level of literacy demand, in how the activity is presented or in how the children record their results;

◗ varying the degree of independence expected, since greater independence tends to present greater challenges;

◗ targeting questions to individuals, so that the level of difficulty of the question is roughly matched to the child's likely ability to answer successfully;

◗ providing suitable resources, which can include additional resources for those requiring extra support and optional resources so they can make their own judgement about whether they need support.
(Adapted from Naylor and Keogh, 1998)

Task
Discuss with teachers in your school how they differentiate science activities to allow all children to achieve the learning objectives.

◗ Which of the above strategies do they use to allow all children (including gifted and talented) to achieve their full potential?
◗ How are the children organised?
◗ Are they working in ability groups?

Using the strategies listed above and any ideas from the teachers in your school, decide on at least two differentiation strategies that you intend to use in your next science lesson. Think about whether and how your planning might need to be adjusted to take these strategies into account.

Implement these strategies in your next science lesson and try to note how the children respond.

Evaluation and follow up
Reflect on how effective your chosen strategies were. To what extent have they helped more of the children to learn effectively? Do they need to be modified to make them more effective? Should they be included in your future planning?

If you have time you can repeat this process with other differentiation strategies and gradually extend the range of approaches that you can use successfully.

Background
By now you will have developed your awareness and understanding of a number of aspects of planning for teaching science. You now need to plan a sequence of lessons on a topic to build into a unit of work.

Preparation
You should have carried out the activities in Progression in ideas, **pages 67–69**.

Use the outline for the short-term planning that is used in the school (many schools now expect their teachers to use a specified format for planning), or you can use Mrs Martineau's plan (**page 25**) which you may have used previously.

Task
Use the medium-term plan to plan a lesson or a short sequence of lessons for teaching a science topic. Plan your lessons using the framework. Try to ensure that you can answer the following questions from your plans:

◗ What ideas are the children likely to have? How will my teaching build from these ideas? Am I planning to achieve progression in their ideas?
◗ What range of teaching and learning strategies will I be using? How will I begin the lesson? What will the children be doing during the lesson? How will I conclude the lesson?
◗ Will the lesson give enough opportunity for the children to develop the skills involved in practical science investigation?
◗ Have I thought about the details of classroom management? Am I clear about grouping? Classroom layout? Use of space? Access to resources? Timing and sequencing? Transition form one activity to another?
◗ How will I make the activity seem purposeful? What range of questions should I use? What differentiation strategies will be useful?
◗ How will the children record and communicate their ideas?
◗ What approach(es) will I use to find out the children's ideas in order to target my teaching?
◗ How will I motivate the children? How will I ensure that I provide access for all the children, not just some?

Evaluation and follow up

When you have taught a couple of lessons on one topic, evaluate the effectiveness of your planning.

Which aspects of your planning seemed to help the lesson to run smoothly and helped the children to achieve your learning objectives? Were any aspects of the lesson problematic? How could your planning have avoided these problems?

Return to Progression in ideas (**page 69**) to complete your evaluation.

Discuss any strengths and weaknesses with your class teacher, mentor or tutor.

Naylor, S and Keogh, B (1998) 'Differentiation', in R. Sherrington (ed.) *ASE guide to primary science education*, pp. 140–7. Hatfield: ASE.
Sharp, J, Peacock, G, Johnsey, R, Simon, S and Smith, R (2002) *Achieving QTS. Primary science: teaching theory and practice.* Exeter: Learning Matters, Chapter 6.

Your achievements

Now that you have carried out these activities you should be able to:

➲ match activities to learning objectives;
➲ use a range of questioning techniques;
➲ use a range of differentiation strategies;
➲ plan for teaching a series of class lessons.

Link to Professional Standards for QTS

The activities in this section address the following Standards for the award of QTS:

1.7; 2.5; 3.1.2; 3.1.3; 3.3.10.

Introduction

In many schools children's recording in science is rather unimaginative. The pressure of accountability to OFSTED makes many teachers think that the children always have to have a written record of what happens in a science investigation. The valuable framework that supports children's planning can easily turn into a laborious structured written record of the investigation, which makes little contribution to children's learning.

In reality there is a wide variety of possible approaches that could be used for recording in science. The benefits of using a variety of recording methods is that the children can more readily view them as purposeful methods of communication, rather than as a written record for its own sake. For example, a class could be germinating seeds and write a record of what they did, what happened and what they found out using a structured recording framework. Alternatively, they could use their new knowledge to write a set of instructions for a seed packet, describing what needs to be done to get the seeds to grow well. Instead of just being a written record, the set of instructions now becomes a purposeful means of communication with which children are more likely to engage positively.

In this section you will observe what range of recording/communicating strategies are used in your school, including the use of ICT, and plan to use and evaluate suitable strategies in your teaching.

Preparation

Review the range of strategies available to use for recording and communicating in science that were identified in Chapter 3 (**page 55**). You may be able to add to this list from further reading.

Create a grid like the one below to help you. Identify appropriate age ranges for using these strategies and think of an example of when you may be able to use it. There are a number of examples already in the table.

Observation of recording and communicating in science		
Approach to recording and communicating	Age range	Example of use
Drawing/labelling a picture	Year 1	E.g. the parts of the human body
Sequencing a set of pictures		
Using a framework to write a report	Year 3	E.g. writing a set of instructions for a seed packet to grow the seeds
Posters		
Displays		
Writing a letter		
Graphs, tables, charts		
Drama	Year 5	E.g. the movement of blood around the body
Discussions		
Concept map		
Using ICT		

Task 1

Look at any science displays in the school and any other examples of children's work in science that you can find.

- What range of recording methods has been used?
- Do some methods seem more effective or more appropriate than others?
- Would you find some methods difficult to use?

Task 2

When you are in school look for examples of children recording results and communicating findings using ICT. It will be useful if you can check what ICT resources are potentially available. Some of the ICT resources you might find in your school are:

- datalogging equipment and software;
- control software;
- digital thermometers;
- databases;
- spreadsheets;
- graphing packages;
- models and simulations;
- word processing programmes;
- multimedia/presentation programmes;
- CD-ROMs;
- Internet.

Do the children have access to any of these resources? Talking to your class teacher or the ICT co-ordinator about the use of ICT in science will help you to identify any possible benefits or obstacles to using ICT resources.

Evaluation and follow up

Reflect on the recording/communicating strategies that you have seen evidence of around the school.

- What have you learnt about the value of some of these strategies?
- What have you learnt about the problems in using some of these strategies?
- What have you learnt about the benefits of using ICT?
- What have you learnt about the obstacles to using ICT?

Where you identify practical difficulties (e.g. lack of ICT resources, lack of time) it will be useful to consider what practical steps you could take to overcome them. Again, further discussion with the class teacher or ICT co-ordinator will be useful.

Preparation
Have the grid of recording and communicating methods (above) available to refer to in your planning.

Task
When you plan a class lesson in science, plan to use a range of methods for children to record the results and/or communicate their findings. Include the use of ICT where this is relevant. How will you organise the children for recording? Will all the children record in the same way? Create a grid like the one below to help you, putting in the recording strategies you intend to try.

Planning for teaching

Method of recording and/or communicating	Possible use of ICT	Factors to consider in planning
Written report		
Annotated or labelled drawing		
Drama		
Graphs or charts		
Poster or display		
Database		

Evaluation and follow up
Reflect on the recording/communicating strategies that you have used in your teaching.

You may find it helpful to create a grid like the one below, to evaluate the recording/communicating strategies that you used or observed.

Evaluation of recording/communicating strategies

Method of recording	Uses ICT?	Potential for assessment?	Difficulties in using this approach	Potential audience for communication
Written report				
Display				
Database				
Graphs				

Ball, S (1998) 'Science and information technology', in R Sherrington (ed.) *ASE guide to primary science education*, pp. 168–74. Hatfield: ASE.
Feasey, R and Gallear, B (2001) *Primary science and Information Communication Technology.* Hatfield: ASE.
Newton, D (2002) *Talking sense in science.* London: Routledge.
Sharp, J, Peacock, G, Johnsey, R, Simon, S and Smith, R (2002) *Primary science: teaching theory and practice.* Exeter: Learning Matters, Chapters 3 and 9.

Your achievements

Now that you have carried out these activities you should be able to:

- ➲ identify a range of useful recording/communicating strategies in science;
- ➲ plan to use a range of recording/communicating strategies;
- ➲ evaluate these in your teaching.

Chapter 4 Assessment and recording in science

Link to Professional Standards for QTS

The activities in this section address the following Standards for the award of QTS:

1.7; 3.1.2; 3.2.1; 3.2.2; 3.2.3.

Introduction

Recent research (such as Black and Wiliam,1998) shows the value of taking children's ideas into account when you are teaching science. Taking children's ideas into account is another way of describing formative assessment. This type of assessment is carried out by teachers as part of their normal teaching, so the children don't think that they are being 'tested' but see themselves as doing the usual kinds of things that they do in the classroom. Quite a variety of formative assessment methods is available when teaching science, so it is possible to be innovative and creative in your teaching even while you are assessing the children. Assessment certainly doesn't have to be more boring tests!

Good formative assessment will help you to have a better idea of where the children are up to, what they have achieved, how much progress they are making and what difficulties they are having. It will also help the children themselves to recognise their own achievements, progress and difficulties and to become more involved in their own learning. This section includes activities to help you to include formative assessment in your planning and to evaluate the formative assessment that you carry out.

Preparation

Look at the assessment policy in the school.

- ➲ What guidance does it give about when and why assessment should take place?
- ➲ Does it give any specific guidance about assessment in science?
- ➲ Does it make suggestions about what formative assessment methods to use in science?
- ➲ Does it suggest any reading or sources of support for assessment in science?

Task

Try to find an opportunity to discuss with other teachers how they go about assessment in science. Ideally you may be able to observe another teacher during a science lesson and then discuss afterwards how s/he made use of any opportunities for assessment.

Evaluation and follow up

Consider what the implications are for you in planning assessment in science.

Preparation

Go back and refresh your memory about the range of methods you could use for formative assessment in science (Chapter 2, **page 31**). You may also want to read more about the range of approaches which are available to use for collecting evidence and making judgements about the children's ideas in science (see Bibliography).

Task

Which of these methods do you think will be most valuable to you?
Which do you think will be easiest to manage in the classroom?

Create a grid like the one below to help you make judgements about which approaches you might use in your teaching.

Comparing approaches to formative assessment		
Approach to assessment	How valuable?	How manageable?
Asking questions		
Listening to the words children use		
Structured drawing		
Structured writing		
Free writing and drawing		
Concept maps		
Grouping, sorting and classifying		
Matching activities		
Structured activities – e.g. true/false		
Concept cartoons		
Children's self-assessment		
Other methods		

Evaluation and follow up

You should be able to make a provisional decision about which approaches you think will be most effective when you are teaching science.

Preparation

When you are planning for science teaching, think about how to include formative assessment in your planning.

Task

Plan for more than one approach to formative assessment so that you develop experience of more than one assessment method. You should include teacher questioning and marking children's work as two of the approaches you build into your planning since these approaches will be central to much of your teaching.

Your planning should include at least one opportunity to assess the children's scientific skills rather than their scientific ideas. This may well involve interacting with the children as they engage in scientific enquiry.

Think about any possible obstacles or difficulties in carrying out your plans. If it is possible, you should discuss your planning for assessment with the class teacher.

When you teach the lesson you should note what seems significant about the children's learning and what the implications might be for your teaching.

Evaluation and follow up

Create a grid like the one below to help you review the formative assessment methods that you used. What are the implications for your future teaching?

Where you identify practical difficulties with using potentially valuable approaches (e.g. concept mapping, which can be valuable but which is not easy to manage), it will be useful to consider what practical steps you could take to make them more manageable. Again, discussion with the class teacher will be useful, as will reading about how to use some of these assessment methods in the classroom.

As for assessment of scientific skills, watching the children, talking to them and looking at how they record their enquiries will provide you with valuable information. You will find it useful to consider how feasible it is to create the time in which you could do this. If it proves very difficult to create suitable opportunities then you may need to look at your approach to classroom organisation and management.

Planning for formative assessment		
Approach to assessment	Potential value for assessment	Difficulties in using this approach
Asking questions		
Listening to the words children use		
Structured drawing		
Structured writing		
Free writing and drawing		
Concept maps		
Grouping, sorting and classifying		
Matching activities		
Structured activities – e.g. true/false		
Concept cartoons		
Children's self-assessment		
Other methods		

Black, P and Wiliam, D (1998) *Inside the black box*. London: Kings College. This pamphlet gives extensive research background about the value of formative assessment.

Harlen, W (2000a) *The teaching of science in primary schools* (3rd Edition). London: David Fulton, Chapters 14–18.

Harlen, W (2000b) *Teaching, learning and assessing science 5–12*. London: Paul Chapman, Chapters 8 and 9.

Keogh, B and Naylor, S (2000) 'Assessment in the early years', in M de Boo (ed.) *Science 3–6: laying the foundations in the early years*, pp. 48–56. Hatfield: ASE.

Naylor, S and Keogh, B (2000) *Concept cartoons in science education*. Sandbach: Millgate House. Concept cartoons are an approach to assessment that naturally leads on to scientific enquiry.

Sharp, J, Peacock, G, Johnsey, R, Simon, S and Smith, R (2002) *Primary science: teaching theory and practice*. Exeter: Learning Matters, Chapter 8.

White, R and Gunstone, R (1992) *Probing understanding*. London: Falmer. Although many of the examples quoted are secondary, this book gives extensive guidance on using a range of assessment methods in science.

Your achievements

Now that you have carried out these activities you should be able to:

- ⊃ consider how a school's assessment policy affects your planning and teaching;
- ⊃ choose a range of strategies for assessing children's learning;
- ⊃ evaluate assessment strategies.

Link to Professional Standards for QTS

The activities in this section address the following Standards for the award of QTS:

1.1; 1.2; 1.3; 1.7; 2.4; 3.1.1; 3.1.2; 3.3.1; 3.3.3; 3.3.5; 3.3.6; 3.14.

Introduction

This chapter addresses issues of inclusion in science and how thinking skills relate to science. Both of these areas are quite subtle and are addressed much more through the approach that a teacher adopts than through the actual content of science lessons. In each case they are noted in the National Curriculum as desirable aims for science teaching. Some teachers feel that the overwhelming weight of content in the National Curriculum means that the emphasis in their teaching is on facts for children to learn and that inclusion and thinking skills come a long way down their list of priorities. However, other teachers would argue that, without addressing inclusion and thinking skills in a serious way, it is unlikely that children will learn the science content effectively anyway. This is something that you will have to make up your own mind about, based on your growing professional experience.

In this section you are invited to review the school's policy and practice and to reflect on your own experience in terms of inclusion and thinking skills.

Preparation
Read the section on other aspects of science education in Chapter 2, **pages 34–36**. Obtain a copy of the school's policy for science.

What references can you find to inclusion and to promoting positive images (including positive images of science itself and positive images of people from different backgrounds engaging in science)?

Are any specific strategies suggested for inclusion, for promoting equal opportunities or for promoting positive images in science?

Task
Look at the text-based and pictorial resources available for science.

- ➲ How is the school's policy implemented in the resources available for science?
- ➲ What kinds of images are presented in the resources available?
- ➲ To what extent do these images help to counter stereotyping, celebrate diversity and promote inclusion (rather than present science as a white, male, European occupation)?

Discuss with the science co-ordinator what the priority issues are for inclusion in science in the school.

- ➲ Are there any specific strategies that the school is trying to adopt in science teaching and learning?

Review your own planning and teaching of science in terms of inclusion.

- ➲ To what extent are you aware of avoiding negative and promoting positive images in science?
- ➲ To what extent do you avoid stereotyping and celebrate cultural diversity in science?
- ➲ To what extent are you aware of how your use of language might exclude some children from engaging fully in science?
- ➲ To what extent do you attempt to adjust your language to ensure that it is as inclusive as possible?

Evaluation and follow up

Reviewing the school's policy, resources and strategies should help to provide you with ideas for practical applications of inclusion principles in science.

Reviewing your own planning and teaching of science should help you to become more aware of these issues and to deal with them more sensitively in your teaching.

Preparation

Obtain a copy of the school's policy for science.

What references can you find to promoting thinking skills through science?

Task

Look at the resources available for science.

➲ How do the resources available for science help to implement the school's policy?

Discuss with the science co-ordinator what the school is aiming for in terms of the links between science and thinking skills.

➲ What specific opportunities are identified in science for promoting thinking skills?
➲ What guidance is available for staff to help them to identify the types of strategies that are likely to promote thinking skills in science?

Review your own planning and teaching of science in terms of thinking skills.

➲ To what extent are you aware of including thinking skills in your planning and teaching?
➲ Do you use any particular strategies to help children to develop thinking skills?
➲ Are there strategies that you have seen other teachers using that you could include in your teaching?
➲ Are there strategies that you have read about that you could include in your teaching?

Evaluation and follow up

Reviewing the school's policy, resources and strategies should help to provide you with ideas to help you to develop thinking skills in science.

Reviewing your own planning and teaching of science should help you to become more aware of the importance of thinking skills and how these can become a priority in your teaching

Peet, G (1998) 'Equal opportunities', in A Cross and G Peet (eds) *Teaching science in the primary school: Book 2*, pp. 59–74. Plymouth: Northcote House.
Smith, A (1995) *Accelerated learning in the classroom*. Stafford: Network Educational Press.
Thorp, S (1991) *Race, equality and science teaching*. Hatfield: ASE.

Your achievements

Now that you have carried out these activities you should be able to:

➲ identify how the school's policy and practice help to promote inclusion in science;
➲ identify how the school's policy and practice help to promote thinking skills through science;
➲ review your own practice in terms of inclusion and thinking skills.

An important part of professional development is review and action planning. Now that you have completed the Developing your Skills phase of your development as a teacher you should review what actions you need to take before moving on to the next phase.

For the activities that you have completed in this chapter, you can use the grid below to summarise your professional development. We recommend that you complete this grid in discussion with your teacher, tutor or other professional colleague. In preparation for the discussion tick the activities that you have completed (we have listed them separately although it is likely that you will have carried them out as one whole experience). Rate your confidence level roughly from low to high. Through discussion you need to decide on the actions you need to take to develop your understanding.

The activities in the next chapter are intended to provide the next level of professional challenge. If you are feeling reasonably confident in any of the areas covered, these activities should be at an appropriate level to provide progression in your learning. However it is important to think about what additional preparation you could do such as reading, attending courses, assessing and developing your own understanding in areas of science that you have not yet taught.

If you are feeling less confident then using some of the strategies above will be essential to ensure that you are able to make appropriate progress. Part of your development may be to work in school to try out some of the activities again in a new context or to engage in further observation of teaching.

Before leaving this chapter you should ensure that you have you have completed any profiling required by your training provider and that you have acquired the appropriate evidence of your achievement of the Standards.

Developing Your Skills – review and action planning grid

Theme	Activities	Confidence Low → High			Action
1 Progression in ideas	• Exploring children's ideas to help to plan effectively				
2 Teaching and learning strategies	• Learning about models and analogies				
3 Teaching practical science	• Learning about teaching practical science to a whole class				
4 Classroom management and resourcing	• Exploring effective management of science with whole classes				
5 Planning and teaching science	• Planning for whole class teaching of science				
6 Children communicating science	• Learning about ways for children to record science				
7 Assessment and recording	• Learning about formative assessment strategies in science				
8 Other aspects of of science education	• Taking account of inclusion and thinking skills				

Chapter 5   **Extending your Skills** ⟳ Introduction

Contents

Introduction	91
Progression in ideas	93
Teaching and learning strategies	96
Teaching practical science	98
Classroom management, organisation and resources	101
Planning and teaching science	104
Children communicating and recording science	107
Assessment and recording in science	110
Other aspects of science education	113
Conclusion	116

Introduction and individual training plan

The activities in this section are for trainee teachers who have had experience of teaching science over a sustained period of time. You will have spent some time teaching science to a whole class and will have taken responsibility for planning and organising the lessons that you taught. It is likely that you will have taught a limited number of areas of science. You will probably need more experience of teaching science to be able to reflect on specific issues that might influence the effectiveness of your teaching. Many of the activities assume that you have also developed your ability to reflect on your own practice. This will enable you to focus on researching your own practice, with or without the support of teachers in the school.

Researching your own practice should start early in your final school placement. You may find it helpful to start this chapter with the final theme, *other aspects of science education* on **page 113**. This will help to give you an insight into how you can use an action research strategy to evaluate and improve your teaching. You will find that you can use this strategy in the other themes in this chapter.

In the grid on page 92 we have identified the activities that you will be carrying out for each theme. Most of the activities are to be carried out in a school setting, although preparation may be done elsewhere. There are spaces in the grid so that you can map out the activities that you will cover and agree with the school as to when and where you will carry them out. This will be your individual training plan (ITP) for the Extending your Skills stage. You may not need to do all of the activities if you have had extensive experience in school already. If time is short you will need to prioritise the activities. You should be able to carry out the activities in this chapter over a six- to eight-week period, working in your base class and teaching much of the science.

You may decide that it would be helpful to observe other teachers to inform your reflections on your own practice. It is essential that this is carried out in a professional manner so that both you and the teacher have agreed the nature and purpose of your observation.

Theme	Page Ref	Activities	Links to other activities	Links to QTS Standards	When and where the activity will be carried out
1 Progression in ideas	p. 93	Learning how to respond to children's misconceptions • Research likely misconceptions • Plan intervention strategies • Try out and evaluate intervention strategies • Make targeted observations in other classes to support aspects of personal learning	All activities should now be carried out within your normal science teaching	1.7; 2.1; 2.3; 3.1.1; 3.1.2	
2 Teaching and learning strategies	p. 96	Learning about specific strategies for teaching science • Extend and justify the range of strategies used • Use a greater range of strategies and evaluate these • Make targeted observations in other classes to support aspects of personal learning	All activities should now be carried out within your normal science teaching	1.7; 2.4; 3.1.1; 3.1.2; 3.1.5; 3.3.3	
3 Teaching practical science	p. 98	Teaching children how to hypothesise, evaluate and engage in critical thinking • Plan for progression in investigative skills • Teach investigative skills and evaluate strategies • Look for evidence of successful learning • Make targeted observations in other classes to support aspects of personal learning	All activities should now be carried out within your normal science teaching	1.7; 3.1.1; 3.1.2	
4 Classroom management, organisation and resources	p. 101	Looking at a chosen aspect of management in your own teaching • Review aspects of management • Become more aware of how other teachers manage science • Look for any impact of selected approaches on learning • Evaluate selected management strategy • Make targeted observations in other classrooms to support aspects of personal learning	All activities should now be carried out within your normal science teaching	1.7; 2.7; 3.1.3; 3.3.1; 3.3.3; 3.3.7; 3.3.8; 3.3.9	
5 Planning and teaching science	p.104	Extending your planning skills and learning more about levels of planning • Identify levels of planning • Make planning more comprehensive • Plan assessment for learning • Link planning and evaluating • Evaluate selected aspects of planning • Make targeted observations in other classrooms to support aspects of personal learning	All activities should now be carried out within your normal science teaching	1.5; 1.6; 1.7; 3.1.1; 3.1.2; 3.1.4; 3.2.1; 3.2.2; 3.3.6	
6 Children communicating and recording science	p. 107	Looking at communicating science through literacy and numeracy • Plan for links with literacy • Plan for links with numeracy • Incorporate aspects of literacy and numeracy into science teaching • Make targeted observations in other classrooms to support aspects of personal learning	All activities should now be carried out within your normal science teaching	1.7; 2.5; 3.1.2; 3.1.3; 3.3.10	
7 Assessment and recording in science	p. 110	Learning about summative and formative assessment in science • Plan for formative assessment • Use suitable formative assessment • Review school policy on summative assessment • Make formative and summative judgements • Plan for recording children's achievement; record and report children's progress • Make targeted observations in other classrooms to support aspects of personal learning	All activities should now be carried out within your normal science teaching	1.7; 3.1.2; 3.2.1; 3.2.2; 3.2.3; 3.2.6; 3.2.7	
8 Other aspects of science education	p. 113	Carrying out classroom-based research to consider inclusion and/or thinking skills • Explore specific issues in practice • Implement action research approach • Make targeted observations in other classrooms to support aspects of personal learning	All activities should now be carried out within your normal science teaching	1.1; 1.2; 1.3; 1.7; 2.4; 3.1.1; 3.1.2; 3.3.1; 3.3.3; 3.3.6; 3.14	

Progression in ideas

Link to Professional Standards for QTS

The activities in this section address the following Standards for the award of QTS:

1.7; 2.1; 2.3; 3.1.1; 3.1.2.

Introduction

By now you will have gained experience of the wide range of ideas that children typically hold and begun to realise how important these are when you are trying to develop their ideas further. The children's ideas should make a difference to your planning. Although you will be required to follow a Scheme of Work, this still has to be interpreted in a way that helps children to modify and develop their ideas.

Their ideas will also make a difference to how you teach, particularly in how you intervene in response to their ideas. Some of your interventions will be for classroom management purposes, but there will also be opportunities to intervene in more productive ways. For example, you might:

⮞ ask children to give a more precise definition of a scientific term;
⮞ ask children to explain their thinking more fully;
⮞ provide more data and challenge the children to explain it;
⮞ offer an alternative viewpoint and invite children to assess which viewpoint is best supported by the evidence;
⮞ ask children to consider whether and how their ideas might apply in a new situation;
⮞ offer an alternative way to interpret the observations they have made;
⮞ provide new information which might clarify their thinking – e.g. explanatory models, new vocabulary or definitions;
⮞ suggest new challenges or opportunities to investigate;
⮞ provide an opportunity for children to communicate their ideas (e.g. through a poster or oral presentation).

These kinds of interventions will help children to clarify their thinking and develop their ideas. They can be used at all stages of a science lesson, from the initial introduction to a final plenary. They may be most valuable in response to children's misconceptions when they arise. However, if you only intervene in response to children' s misconceptions then they will soon learn the rule that *teacher intervention = I've got it wrong!* Interventions should be used to challenge and extend the thinking of all the children, not just those with misconceptions.

This section is intended to help you to focus specifically on how you respond to the children's ideas while you are engaged in your normal teaching. The aim should be that a process of anticipating and responding to children's ideas should become a normal part of your science teaching. It builds on the activity you carried out in Chapter 4, **page 68**.

In this section you will:

⮞   look at children's likely misconceptions and how their ideas might progress;
⮞   think about how you might respond to the misconceptions;
⮞   try out intervention strategies in your teaching;
⮞   reflect on the effectiveness of the intervention strategies.

Preparation

Obtain suitable reference material that gives you background about what the children's ideas are likely to be in the topic(s) you will be teaching, such as Driver *et al.* (1985), Driver *et al.* (1994) and Nuffield (1993).

Find out about the areas of confusion and possible misconceptions that children are likely to have in this topic. Engaging in this process will help you to reflect on your own understanding before you start teaching a topic and to be more alert to misconceptions when they arise in your teaching.

Look at the school Scheme of Work for the lessons you will be teaching, paying particular attention to the learning objectives. What guidance does it give about how children's ideas should progress in the topic? Do you anticipate any difficulties with the expected progression in children's ideas? If so, how might your teaching help to minimise these difficulties?

Now that you have identified likely misconceptions that children in your class might hold, think through ways of responding in order to help their ideas to progress. The table below provides an example from Mrs Martineau's class. Jess thinks that the more water there is, the more it will push up and tries to use the word 'upthrust' to explain this.

Identifying and responding to misconceptions and developing intervention strategies	
Jess: '*I think the boat goes higher in the deep water. It's because the upthrust gets bigger when there is more water.*'	
Intervention strategy	**Mrs Martineau's response**
Ask children to give a more precise definition of a scientific term	Tell me more about what you think upthrust means, Jess
Ask children to explain their thinking more fully	Tell me some more about why you think that, Jess
Provide more data and challenge the children to explain it	Elana's group said that they could not see any difference in the way that the boat floated, whatever the depth of the water
Offer an alternative viewpoint and invite children to assess which viewpoint is best supported by the evidence	That's really puzzling, Jess, because when I take my children on the boats in the park it doesn't seem to make any difference whether we were in the deep part or the shallow part of the lake. I wonder why that is?
Ask children to consider whether and how their ideas might apply in a new situation	What do you think would happen if a boat went into very deep water? Would upthrust get so big that the boat would come out of the water?
Offer an alternative way to interpret the observations they have made	Can we think of any other reasons why the boat was higher in the deeper water? Did we check whether the weight of the boat was the same when we floated it in different depths of water?
Provide new information which might clarify their thinking – e.g. explanatory models, new vocabulary or definitions	Upthrust is an interesting word, Jess. We haven't talked about that yet in class, have we? You only have upthrust when something is pressing down in the water. It is a force pushing back. Do you remember what we said about balanced forces? You push down on the chair and it pushes back with the same force. If the chair could push back harder than you push down, it would be like an ejector seat and I would have a class full of children jumping up and down all the time! Water is the same. When a boat is floating the push up (upthrust) is the same as the boat pushing down. Let's see how that fits with what you were thinking
Suggest new challenges or opportunities to investigate	Why not try pushing a balloon into different depths of water Jess?
Provide an opportunity for children to communicate their ideas (e.g. through a poster or oral presentation)	Jess's group and Elana's group are going to tell us what they think. They have come up with some different ideas

Task

Look for opportunities to find out as much as you can about the children's ideas. This will include opportunities while you are teaching, such asking them questions, class discussion, listening to group discussions, providing opportunities for children to ask their own questions and so on. It will also include any outcomes of their learning, such as drawings, written work, annotated drawings, posters and concept maps.

Creating and using these kinds of opportunities enable you to become more aware of children's areas of confusion and misconceptions. Increasing your awareness in this way helps you to plan and teach more effectively.

When you are aware of possible areas of confusion or misconceptions try out some of the response strategies that you have thought about above. How do the children respond?

You can then consider:

- Which types of intervention seem to be the most productive?
- Do children appear to respond more positively to some types of interventions than to others?
- Do your interventions seem to have any impact on how the children's ideas develop?
- Can you see any ways to improve your interventions?

Evaluation and follow up

Promoting progression in the children's ideas is a challenge for all teachers, no matter how experienced they are. By now you should be able to recognise some of the vital factors in making any headway in this area. These factors include:

- having a reasonably clear sense of what progression looks like;
- planning in a way that recognises children's existing ideas and takes these into account;
- using informal methods of assessment that help to provide access to the children's ideas;
- developing suitable intervention strategies in response to the children's ideas.

Developing your understanding of each of these factors may not be sufficient to guarantee that your children will make good progress, but it will make that far more likely.

Driver, R, Guesne, E, and Tiberghien, A (eds) (1985) *Children's ideas in science*. Milton Keynes: Open University.
Driver, R, Squires, A, Rushworth, P and Wood-Robinson, V (1994) *Making sense of secondary science*. London: Routledge.
Various authors (1993) *Nuffield Primary Science Teachers' Guides*. London: Collins Educational.

Your achievements

Now that you have completed these activities you should be able to:

- research children's misconceptions and likely progression in their ideas and use this to anticipate ways of responding to children's ideas;
- respond to, challenge and develop children's ideas using appropriate intervention strategies;
- evaluate the effectiveness of intervention strategies for challenging children's misconceptions and helping their ideas to progress.

Chapter 5 — Teaching and learning strategies

Link to Professional Standards for QTS

The activities in this section address the following Standards for the award of QTS:

1.7; 2.4; 3.1.1; 3.1.2; 3.1.5; 3.3.3.

Introduction

By now you will have tried and tested several teaching and learning strategies in science and other areas of the curriculum. It is likely that you will have had opportunities to instruct and explain to children, and you will find suggestions on whole class science teaching in the section on Teaching practical science. This leaves us with the following:

Training children in the use of science equipment, both manual and ICT tools
Training children to use equipment is of lesser importance than other strategies, but it is for this reason that practising this strategy is so often left out. Nevertheless, whether you are introducing young children to thermometers, microscopes and stopwatches or older children to light and temperature sensors, they need time and structured opportunities to explore and use these safely and competently. Children can have a great sense of excitement and delight in acquiring knowledge and skills. Training children to use tools meets science and maths objectives of measuring carefully, developing and practising fine motor skills, co-operative social skills and language skills of negotiation and agreement.

Choosing strategies to help individual children with special needs
Prioritising time with a chosen child or group will inevitably mean less attention for the rest of the class. All teachers do this – the trick is to find a balance between whole class, small group and individual attention. Good organisation is the key to success. Give the class a range of interesting activities that will not require too much teacher attention, and assure them that they will have your time and attention in the plenary. This will free you to work closely with each child with SEN. The rewards can be great for the child, you and the class: the child will develop science skills and knowledge in a well-supported environment, you can diagnose learning needs and the class learns patience and independent behaviour.

Taking children on an outdoor visit or inviting a visitor into school
Taking the children on a visit or receiving a visitor can be as much a social experience as a scientific one. Ensuring the visit's success as a scientific experience not only requires good planning and organisation but also being very clear about the science objectives. As well as informing parents, the adults who accompany you and your class will need relevant information prepared for them in advance. The start of the visit may be busy and you will have little time to ensure that the supporting adults have the necessary information, which might include:

➲ the learning objectives (simple and few);
➲ useful questions to ask the children;
➲ a timetable and a meeting place in case groups get separated;
➲ recommendations about souvenir purchases, if appropriate.

Preparation
You should select an activity that is appropriate to your needs.

1 **Training in the use of scientific/mathematical equipment:**
➲ Look at the science resources for measuring and testing, including ICT, and discuss their use with the science co-ordinator.

○ Practise using the equipment yourself and check that everything is working. It is better to find out if some tools are defective now than give them to children who may assume that *they* have broken the equipment or that they are inadequate in using the tools.

○ Choose informal measurements or investigations, such as the time taken to go to and from the cloakroom, the temperature in different places in the classroom or outside, looking at tiny seeds or the texture of different fabrics through the microscope, etc.

2 **Children with Special Educational Needs:**

○ Read the school policy for science, noting particularly the school's declared aims for children learning science and what support is recommended for children with SEN, whether physical, behavioural or language. Are teachers able to put the policy into practice?

○ Discuss with the SEN co-ordinator and your class teacher what approaches you might use in science with the targeted children with special needs.

3 **A school visit or visitor:**

○ Organise an outside visit or invite a visitor into school. Ask the advice of the science co-ordinator on venues and visitors that the school has used to enhance children's learning.

○ Work through the following matrix to plan the visit.

Planning a school visit/visitor – a check list			
School Policy check Notes Completed	Discussion with the class teacher and/or science co-ordinator – arrange travel if necessary Notes Completed	Carry out risk assessment and consider Health and Safety. Make a prior visit to the venue Notes Completed	Cater for children with Special Needs Notes Completed
Notify parents as appropriate Notes Completed	Plan ratio of adults and arrange support Notes Completed	Plan the resources required, including materials for children's recording Notes Completed	Write out information and objectives for adult helpers Notes Completed

Task

Carry out your chosen teaching strategy.

1 **Training in the use of scientific/mathematical equipment:**
Plan a science lesson, taking the above into account. Justify the way that you intend to work and criteria to evaluate the effectiveness of your practice. This should include evidence of successful learning. Discuss this with the science co-ordinator and your class teacher.

2 **Children with Special Educational Needs:**
Plan a science lesson, taking the above into account. Justify the way that you intend to work and criteria to evaluate the effectiveness of your practice. This should include evidence of successful learning. Discuss this with the SEN co-ordinator and your class teacher.

3 **A school visit or visitor:**
Plan a science lesson, taking the above into account. Justify the way that you intend to work and criteria to evaluate the effectiveness of your practice. This should include evidence of successful learning. Discuss this with the science co-ordinator and your class teacher.

Evaluation and follow up

Reflect on the effectiveness of your strategy from your point of view and that of the child and any adults who were involved in the activity. Use the criteria that you identified earlier to help with your analysis.

After you have made your own notes discuss with your class teacher and/or the science co-ordinator and/or SEN co-ordinator what you have learnt about the strategy from this teaching experience. It will be helpful if they have been using the same criteria that you identified at the start of the activity.

Your achievements

Harlen, W (2000) *The teaching of science in primary schools* (3rd Edition). London: David Fulton, Chapter 10.

Now that you have completed these activities you should be able to:

○ become aware of successful strategies employed by other teachers;
○ extend the range of strategies that you employ;
○ justify the way the strategy was implemented;
○ look for evidence of successful learning;
○ evaluate your practice, using criteria that you have devised for yourself;
○ discuss the effectiveness of your practice with other colleagues, using your criteria.

Chapter 5   Teaching practical science

Link to Professional Standards for QTS

The activities in this section address the following Standards for the award of QTS:

1.7; 3.1.1; 3.1.2.

Introduction

You should by now have had experience of planning for practical science. You should also be aware of the key processes and skills needed to carry out effective investigations. These include:

- identifying the problem to be investigated;
- raising questions;
- making predictions;
- planning the investigation;
- fair testing;
- observation and measurement;
- collecting and recording data systematically;
- explanations/hypotheses;
- critical reflection/evaluation;
- communication.

There are two activities in this theme. In the first, you consider the progression of children's understanding of scientific investigations in planning for science. In the second activity, you focus specifically on explanations and hypotheses and critical reflection and evaluation.

Progression in investigative skills

Background

This activity should be carried out when you are planning for your science teaching.

In your planning you will need to take account of the development of the children's abilities in these areas. Just as you need to support progression in children's conceptual understanding of science, you also need to support the development of procedural understanding. Progression in procedural understanding can be seen through an increasing depth of understanding of scientific processes and the ability to work independently to apply that understanding.

It is possible to map out how children's understanding of scientific procedures might progress. For example, in fair testing, progression might include:

- carrying out a simple fair test with the teacher's help;
- understanding, in discussion with the teacher, when a simple fair test is needed;
- understanding when a fair test is needed without the teacher's help;
- knowing how to vary one factor while keeping others the same;
- recognising the key factors involved and taking them into account in investigations where fair testing is needed.

You will find examples of progression in scientific skills in Goldsworthy and Feasey (1997).

Children will initially need your support to learn how to carry out scientific investigations. This is not something that they can discover on their own. Whatever the age of the children, whenever they are learning a new skill you will need to give them support until you feel that they can work independently. Similarly, when they are learning how to plan and carry out a complete investigation, initially they will need support to decide what their questions might be, what steps to take to answer the question, how to record their findings and how to draw conclusions and communicate their ideas.

You will find that some teachers are very effective at helping the children to carry out investigations, particularly fair testing, but are less effective at enabling their children to engage in the initial stages of identifying the problem. Some children merely carry out investigations following the teacher's instructions or are heavily directed by the teacher. Similarly, some children are not encouraged to reflect on and review their work.

In order for you to teach science investigations effectively you need to ensure that you think about what the children can currently do on their own and what they will need your support to do. You may be surprised at how much young children will be able to do on their own.

The table below illustrates what Mrs Martineau's decision-making in scientific investigations might have looked like. You can see from this that, although most of the children carried out the investigation on their own, there were some aspects where Mrs Martineau gave support to the whole class and some where she focused on a group of children. In this lesson the children were able to carry out a whole investigation within the lesson but the focus was on recording.

Mrs Martineau's decision-making in scientific investigations		
Skills	**Teacher's role**	**Children's role**
Identifying the problem to be investigated	Gave children concept cartoon to identify a problem	Children discuss the problem
Raising questions	Support discussion where required	Children raise questions through discussion
Making predictions	Support discussion where required	Some children will predict what would happen before investigating. I will ask others what they think
Planning the investigation	Support planning where necessary	All children able to plan what to do and how to do it
Fair testing	Some children may need help to decide which factor to change	Most children should now be able to fair test
Observation and measurement	Support where necessary but probably need to target Yasmin's group	All children should now be able to observe and measure
Collect and record data systematically (main focus for the lesson)	Need to target Yasmin's group to ensure effective records are kept	Remainder of the class should be fine
Explanations/hypotheses	Need to support the discussion	Some children are beginning to do this without support
Critical reflection/evaluation	Need to support the discussion	Some children are beginning to do this without support
Communication	Support Yasmin's group in deciding how to communicate their findings to the rest of the class	All groups to feed back and most will produce independent written record

Preparation
Identify in the medium-term planning what the learning objectives are for science investigations for the time that you are teaching the class.

You will have decisions to make about whether you are targeting specific skills or are trying to help the children develop the process of investigating as a whole. It is not possible in every lesson to carry out long detailed investigations. Some lessons will require a whole scientific investigation whereas other lessons will draw on specific skills. This should be clear in the school's plans. If not, discuss this with the science co-ordinator or the class teacher.

Task
Using the table, think through which skills you are going to develop and which the children may already know. Think about your role and how it will differ for different skills and for different children. Try to avoid assuming that all children will need to investigate the same thing in the same way. When will you be encouraging the children to work independently and when will you need to give support in using a new skill?

Evaluation and follow up
Discuss your ideas with your teacher or the science co-ordinator. Modify your thinking in the light of the discussion. You should use these ideas to inform your planning.

Planning and teaching investigative skills

Background
This activity should be carried out when you are planning for your science teaching.

Developing explaining/hypothesising
Thinking of explanations or hypotheses is a creative act and this skill begins in the early years. Some teachers do not ask children to explain their results on the basis that their explanations may be unscientific. However, even young children begin to use the word 'because' appropriately and, with practice and encouragement, children quickly become adept at offering explanations and hypotheses that take the evidence and their experience into account. Your role in encouraging explanations is to ask *'Why do you think that happened?'* followed by *'Could there be another reason?'* or *'Or?'* Such questions develop children's thinking skills and illustrate the scientific view of alternative theories for a phenomenon. You can ask children verbally or include a challenge in a writing frame: *'I think this happened because …'* Children who are not asked to explain, generally do not. It can be difficult for children to expose their uncertain ideas to a potentially critical audience. They need positive encouragement.

Developing critical thinking/evaluating
This is higher order thinking and you can encourage this during – and particularly at the end of – an investigation with questions such as *'What other resources could you use? How do you know if the investigation went well? How could it be done differently or better next time?'* Such questions place the emphasis on the investigation, not the individual or group, and remove the stigma of having 'done it wrong'. In many cases, there will be no opportunity to repeat the experiment/s but the critical thinking process will be reinforced and the uncertainties of practical science, especially primary science, are revealed. As with hypothesising, this can be encouraged verbally or within a writing frame: *'If we did this again, we would …'*

It is important that you have high expectations as well as patience. Critical thinking can be difficult for children who fear criticism. It can take time for some children to learn that they are not the target of criticism but are being invited to criticise the experimental factors themselves.

Preparation
Identify a lesson (or series of lessons) where the children will engage in scientific investigation.

Select a teaching approach that is appropriate for the class and one that you feel is easily manageable so that you can spend some time focusing on the issues above.

When planning the lesson think specifically about encouraging children's skills in explaining, hypothesising, evaluating and/or critical thinking. Prepare a range of questions or activities that will encourage your chosen objective. Think particularly about how the plenary might be used to develop these skills. At what other times in your lesson will they occur?

Discuss your learning objectives and choices with the class teacher and science co-ordinator.

Task
Carry out the science lesson as planned.

Evaluation and follow up
Enlist your teacher's help to identify what evidence there is that your strategies had an impact on the children's engagement in explaining, hypothesising, evaluation and/or critical reflection. What evidence do you have of successful learning of practical skills and these skills in particular?

Plan your next steps to continue to develop these skills.

de Boo, M (1999) *Enquiring children, challenging teaching: investigating primary science*. Buckingham: Open University Press.
Fisher, R (1990) *Teaching children to think*. London: Simon & Schuster.
Goldsworthy, A and Feasey, R (1997) *Making sense of primary science investigations*. Hatfield: ASE.
Harlen, W (2000) *The teaching of science in primary schools* (3rd Edition). London: David Fulton, Chapter 20.

Your achievements

Now that you have completed these activities you should be able to:

⊃ plan for progression in science investigations;
⊃ encourage children to develop the skills of explaining, hypothesising, critical thinking and evaluating;
⊃ look for evidence of progression in science investigations.

Classroom management, organisation and resources

Link to Professional Standards for QTS

The activities in this section address the following Standards for the award of QTS:

1.7; 2.7; 3.1.3; 3.3.1; 3.3.3; 3.3.7; 3.3.8; 3.3.9.

Introduction

Experienced teachers appear to be almost instinctive about the way that they manage their teaching. Once the initial decisions have been made about the arrangement of the class for science and resources have been organised it might be assumed that few additional decisions are made. This belies the complex decisions that teachers need to make even when they are confident in the way they organise and manage their class for science. Effective teachers will make lesson-by-lesson decisions about what they need to do to make the lesson effective for the children.

Before you engage in this activity you should be gaining in confidence in your knowledge about which classroom management strategies you feel are likely to be successful and be able to select strategies according to what you are hoping to achieve in a particular lesson.

If you are, you should now be able to consider the implications of these strategies in terms of your other goals for teaching and learning in science – e.g. taking children's ideas into account, developing the skills of scientific investigation, meeting children's specific needs. The decisions that you make about any of these issues will depend on factors such as your previous assessment of the children's learning in science and your awareness of their interests, language and cultural backgrounds.

In this activity you will consider one or a group of issues related to the management and organisation of science lessons. You may decide to carry this out as a small-scale research process. If so then read the section on Other aspects of science education in this chapter (**page 113**) before you start.

Effective management and organisation of science lessons

Effective management and organisation of the classroom is central to many issues in science teaching. Not only will it have an impact on the behaviour of the children, but it can also influence the way that the children perceive science and their engagement in learning science. If we look at Mrs Martineau's class it is obviously organised so that children can work independently of the teacher when appropriate. The children work co-operatively and are encouraged to see learning science as a social rather than a solitary activity. In the one lesson the different organisational strategies allowed for a range of approaches to learning science. It was obvious that the children were highly motivated to learn science and had a positive attitude towards scientific ideas.

Preparation
Read the section in Chapter 2 on Classroom management, organisation and resources (**page 19**).

Task
Think about the strategies for teaching science that you have seen or have experienced as a learner of science. Now that you have had more experience of science and understand more about the teaching

of science, how would you complete the grid below? Which strategies would you put in each cell? After completing the grid, talk to other teachers in the school and ask them which strategies they would put where.

Evaluating strategies		
	Helps children to be more independent and effective science learners	**Causes children to be less independent and ineffective science learners**
Easy to manage		
Hard to manage		

Evaluation and follow up
Consider the following questions:

⮑ Are there any strategies that you might have initially put in the hard to manage cell but, now that you are more experienced, can be put in the easy/effective cell?

⮑ Are there any easy to manage strategies that you now realise should be in the ineffective cell?

⮑ Are there some strategies that other teachers feel are easy to manage and effective that you have put elsewhere? Should you think about finding ways to develop those strategies?

⮑ Are there some strategies that you think are ineffective but that other teachers think are effective? Why do you think that might be?

Your aim should be to build up your repertoire of easy to manage and effective strategies. This might be achieved by modifying the way you organise hard and effective strategies to make them easier and by looking for ways of making easy ineffective strategies more effective.

Preparation
This activity should help you to develop a more in-depth view of management and organisational strategies.

Think about questions that relate to the decisions that you have to make when planning for science teaching. For example:

⮑ Should I group the children by their linguistic ability?

⮑ Should the children be organised in other ability groups for science?

⮑ Which organisational sequence creates the best opportunity to take children's ideas into account? Should there always be a whole class discussion first?

⮑ How can I organise groups to take account of children with English as an additional language? Should these children work together as a group?

⮑ How do I organise the class if the children have different ideas about an area of science? Do I group them according to their ideas?

⮑ What strategies would enable children to function more independently as learners in science?

Can you add any more questions to your list?

Task
Select one of the above issues as a specific focus. Try to keep it relatively simple. Plan a science lesson where you think about how you might address this issue. For example, you might want to find out whether it is better to organise the groups by their ideas or to have a mixture of ideas and understandings in one group. You would need to set up a situation where you tried both kinds of groupings, either within the same lesson or in different lessons. You would need to select criteria for making decisions such as those illustrated below.

You will find it helpful if someone else can observe the lesson, focusing on this specific issue. They can then give you their evaluation of the effectiveness of the strategy you are using.

Detailed analysis of classroom management/organisational strategies

	Time on task	Involvement of all members of the group	Level of discussion	Motivation	Quality of outcomes	Quality of learning
Same ideas						
Mixed ideas						

Evaluation and follow up

Summarise what you see as the most significant aspects of what you have learnt about the issue that you selected. Consider whether there are any changes that you feel you should make in how you manage the organisation of science teaching and learning. Build this into your future planning.

Harlen, W (1999) *Effective teaching of science: a review of research.* Edinburgh: SCRE.
Hodson (1998) *Teaching and learning in science.* Buckingham: Open University.

Your achievements

Now that you have completed these activities you should be able to:

➲ identify specific aspects of classroom management and organisation that you can improve;
➲ consider strategies that are employed by other teachers;
➲ use a greater range of techniques;
➲ evaluate the impact of the strategies that you have employed.

Chapter 5 — Planning and teaching science

Link to Professional Standards for QTS

The activities in this section address the following Standards for the award of QTS:

1.5; 1.6; 1.7; 3.1.1; 3.1.2; 3.1.4; 3.2.1; 3.2.2; 3.3.6.

Introduction

Planning for science can involve a lot of people and as a trainee teacher you may only get to see a part of the whole picture. Although the science co-ordinator may be directly responsible for constructing the long-term plan (or Scheme of Work) for science, it is usual for all the staff in a school to have a say in how it is constructed. Medium-term plans (for one or more year groups) may be put together by a single teacher for each class or they may be shared among small year group or Key Stage teams. Finally, the short-term (or lesson) plans are normally produced by individual teachers, often working in conjunction with learning assistants to plan for individual children's needs where necessary.

This section encourages you to look critically at your planning for science. The activities deal with different levels of planning, making planning more comprehensive, adapting planning, and linking planning and evaluating.

Levels of planning

Preparation
Ask your class teacher or the science co-ordinator for a copy of the school's long-term plans for science. The school may use the QCA Scheme of Work as a long-term plan. Look at how the plans are constructed across the different age ranges. Obtain a copy of your class teacher's medium-term plans and an example of a lesson plan.

Task
Look at how the long-, medium- and short-term plans fit together. You should be able to see how topics are revisited, how many topics are revisited at different ages and how progression in different concepts is mapped through the science curriculum. How are the plans modified if the school has mixed age groups? Can you see the logic of how certain topics are taught at certain times (e.g. flowering plants in spring time)?

Look also at the different kinds of things that are included in the different levels of planning. You should see that the focus shifts from the science concepts in the long-term plans to how children's learning is supported in the short-term.

Look particularly carefully at lesson plans. Are you confident that you include in your lesson planning everything that is expected by the school? Check with the science coordinator that your lesson plans fit with the school's medium-term plans.

Evaluation and follow up
Does your lesson planning need to be modified in any way to take the school's expectations into account?

Making your planning more comprehensive

Preparation

This activity follows on from the final activity in Planning and teaching science in Chapter 4 (planning a sequence of lessons, **page 80**). It will be useful to go back and review this activity and look at Mrs Martineau's planning.

Task

Skim quickly through the other sections in this chapter – they all raise issues and identify aspects of science teaching and learning that you need to recognise in your planning. However, your plans still need to be a sensible length – you can't afford to spend two hours writing out a five-page plan for a single lesson!

As a minimum, your lesson plans should normally make some reference to:

- ⮱ the National Curriculum;
- ⮱ your learning objectives;
- ⮱ how these relate to children's previous learning or experience;
- ⮱ the lesson sequence, including key questions to be used;
- ⮱ the teaching and learning approach(es) to be used, including how to engage and motivate the children and how to be inclusive;
- ⮱ differentiation;
- ⮱ aspects of classroom organisation and health and safety issues;
- ⮱ your assessment focus and the assessment methods to be used.

Review your lesson plans for science so far and check whether they need to be extended.

Check with your teacher or the science coordinator that they feel your planning is effective.

Evaluation and follow up

Is your time being spent on the most important aspects of planning?

Does your lesson planning need to be modified in any way to make your plans more comprehensive?

Adapting planning

Background

We have written about planning for science as though all of this planning could be done in advance of the teaching. This isn't true! The long- and medium-term plans certainly can be written, used and re-used over a number of years. The short-term plans (that is, daily and weekly lesson plans) are just that – short term. Even when a sequence of lessons has been planned to teach a topic, the effective teacher will constantly modify those short-term plans to take into account the responses of the children and any assessment of their understanding. If at the beginning of a new topic the teacher finds that the children have less or more understanding than anticipated then the lesson plans will need to be modified. You should be cautious of planning too many lessons at the start of a topic.

Preparation

You should have planned a sequence of lessons that includes using formative assessment to find out about children's ideas.

Task

When you have taught and evaluated the first lesson, reflect on what you now know about the children's level of understanding. Does your planning now need to be modified at all? Can you move on quickly through some sections because the children are more confident than you expected? Do some aspects need consolidation before you can teach what you had expected to teach? Do certain children need additional support or challenge?

If your plans do need to be modified this does not mean you need to write out whole lesson plans again, but you may need to add notes to your original plans.

Evaluation and follow up

Modify your lesson plans as necessary to take into account what you have found out about the ideas the children hold. You may also need to annotate or modify your medium-term plans. Where the planning–teaching–learning–assessment–planning cycle is more obvious, reflect on how your teaching of science compares with your teaching of literacy.

Repeat the process as you go through your sequence of lessons.

Linking planning and evaluating

Background

In the same way that planning, teaching, learning and assessment form a cycle, so too do planning, teaching, learning and evaluation. The first cycle focuses on what the children are learning; the second cycle focus on what you are learning professionally. So, just as assessing the children should lead to your plans being adjusted, so too should evaluating your teaching.

Preparation

Collect examples of your earlier evaluations of your science teaching, from a previous placement if necessary.

Task

Look back through your earlier evaluations.

➲ What links can you see between your evaluations and your later planning?
➲ Have your plans been modified as a result of previous evaluations?
➲ Do your evaluations include some reference to the teaching approach that you used?
➲ Do your evaluations attempt to identify broader issues in your teaching (such as children's independence) as well as more specific aspects of teaching?
➲ Do your evaluations include how successful your teaching has been in terms of whether the children have achieved your learning objectives?

Evaluation and follow up

Do you need to modify or extend your evaluations to make them as productive as they might be for your professional learning?

Sharp, J, Peacock, G, Johnsey, R, Simon, S and Smith, R (2002) *Achieving QTS. Primary science: teaching theory and practice.* Exeter: Learning Matters, Chapter 6.

Your achievements

Now that you have carried out these activities you should be able to:

➲ contribute to different levels of planning within the school;
➲ produce more comprehensive plans;
➲ modify your planning as a result of formative assessment;
➲ modify your planning as a result of evaluating your teaching.

Chapter 5 — Children communicating and recording science

Link to Professional Standards for QTS

The activities in this section address the following Standards for the award of QTS:

1.7; 2.5; 3.1.2; 3.1.3; 3.3.10.

Introduction

One of the drawbacks of the way that the National Curriculum is organised and inspected is that it emphasises the separateness of the subjects. Even at secondary level this creates some problems; at primary level it makes it much more difficult for teachers to think and work creatively across subject boundaries. Even though children don't naturally think or learn in subject disciplines, they also come to accept the subject boundaries and do not expect skills or knowledge to be transferred from one subject setting to another.

Until the National Curriculum is restructured it is difficult for teachers to avoid working in subjects. However, one way to reduce the impact of the subject boundaries is to create links across subjects where possible. Links between science and literacy, and between science and numeracy, can help to bridge this gap between the subjects.

In this section you will look at the learning objectives in the National Frameworks in order to identify links between science and literacy/numeracy, then build these curriculum links into your teaching.

Linking science and literacy

Preparation

Look at the school's medium-term plans for literacy across a range of year groups. Try to identify areas of the literacy curriculum that have links with science. For example, the National Literacy Strategy for Year 5 Term 2 Non-fiction includes:

1   Non-chronological reports – this could include describing how different objects produce sounds of different pitch or classifying materials as solids, liquids and gases.
2   Explanations – this could include an explanation of how night and day occur.

The table below gives examples of science contexts for each non-fiction genre.

Add your own ideas to the chart. Identify from the school's long-term plans when various classes cover certain topics in science and how these could be matched to plans for literacy.

Links between science and literacy	
Text type and purpose	**Examples of use in science**
Recount – to retell for information or entertainment	• Recount of eggs hatching • Diary of a broad bean
Explanation – to explain a process or how something works	• The water cycle • How rocks are formed • How to make a magnet
Discussion – presents all sides of an issue	• Use of animals in scientific experimentation • Eating for health and eating for entertainment
Non-chronological report – to report or classify	• Describe the function of the human heart • Sorting and classifying alive and not alive
Instruction or procedural – to describe how something is done – to help the reader achieve certain goals	• Instructions for carrying out an experiment • Recipes
Persuasion – to persuade the reader to the author's point of view	• Recycling is your responsibility • The importance of food hygiene

Task

➲ Find literacy resources that use science as the context for learning different genres. Identify Big Books that you can use as whole class texts. Make a list of resources that you identify, for future use.

➲ Plan to teach a literacy lesson that uses science as the context for teaching non-fiction. Relate this to the unit of science that the class is learning about at this time. For example, if they are learning about electricity in science then find a text for literacy that is about electricity (Nuffield Primary Science, 1998, *More About Electricity and Magnetism*, for example). Identify the literacy objectives that can be taught from a science text.

➲ Plan and teach a science/literacy lesson that has specific objectives for recording and communicating children's ideas using a non-fiction framework that the children have learnt about in the literacy hour. For example, they may have learnt how to construct an explanation using a writing frame. The objective of the lesson will be to write an explanation of the science process that they are learning about – for example, how evaporation occurs. (First Steps, 1998, has some useful ideas.)

Evaluation and follow up

As you become more aware of the types of links that can be made between science and literacy you will start to develop ideas and notice resources that help to make this connection, which you can store for future use in your teaching. If you review your teaching, you are likely to find examples of links that you could have made if you had been more aware of this possibility.

Linking science and numeracy

Preparation

Looking at various age ranges, identify areas of the National Numeracy Strategy teaching programmes that address skills that will be utilised in recording for science. You will find some ideas in the NNS Section 5 and 6 Supplement of Examples. You will be able to think of other contexts for yourself. Make a table like the one below to record possible science contexts that you could use for teaching the areas of data handling in each year group.

Links between science and literacy				
Year	**NNS page no.**	**Question**	**Skill used**	**Science topic**
4	114	Do many children get measles nowadays?	Tally chart	Ourselves
4	114	It is said that thrushes are becoming less common. Are there any around our school?	Pictogram	Habitats
5	117	Investigate room temperature using a sensor	Draw and interpret a line graph	

Task

Plan and teach a science lesson using one of the ideas from your chart above. Identify your science learning objectives and the possible numeracy links from the NNS. For example, when learning about dissolving, the science learning objectives for the lesson could be that children should:

- plan and do a simple investigation, choosing appropriate equipment;
- record the results in a chart;
- understand the meaning of dissolving;
- understand saturation.

The numeracy objectives for your lesson would be that children should:

- use a measuring cylinder accurately;
- measure weight accurately;
- record results in a chart;
- draw and interpret a line graph.

Evaluation and follow up

As you become more aware of the types of links that can be made between science and numeracy you will start to develop ideas and notice resources that help to make this connection which you can store for future use in your teaching. If you review your teaching you are likely to find examples of links that you could have made if you had been more aware of this possibility.

Feasey, R (1998) *Primary science and literacy.* Hatfield: ASE.
Feasey, R and Gallear, B (2000) *Primary science and numeracy.* Hatfield: ASE.
First Steps (1998) *Writing: resource book.* Australia: Rigby Heinemann.
Nuffield Primary Science (1998) *Science and literacy. A guide for primary teachers.* London: Collins Educational.

Your achievements

Now that you have completed these activities you should be able to:

- identify possible links between science and literacy;
- identify possible links between science and numeracy;
- include links between science and literacy and science and numeracy in your teaching.

Link to Professional Standards for QTS

The activities in this section address the following Standards for the award of QTS:

1.7; 3.1.2; 3.2.1; 3.2.2; 3.2.3; 3.2.6; 3.2.7.

Introduction

As you come towards the end of your professional preparation for teaching you will need to extend the range of purposes for which you carry out assessments in science. You will continue to use formative assessment, applying a range of methods. You will also need to assess children systematically, keep records of their progress, report on their progress to parents and other teachers, carry out diagnostic assessments, make summative assessment judgements and possibly prepare children for National Tests.

As you extend the range of purposes for which you carry out assessment in science you will probably also need to extend the range of assessment methods that you use regularly in your teaching. The methods that you have already used will still be valuable, but they may not be sufficient for the variety of types of assessment that you now wish to build into your teaching. This section is aimed at helping you to form a more holistic view of assessment in the school.

There are three activities with one evaluation and follow up, which is to be completed at the end of the placement.

In the first activity you will review your experience of assessment and then look at how you can make assessment more specific in your planning. The second activity focuses on the school policy and begins to raise your awareness of summative assessment. The final activity is aimed at recording assessment information and using it to produce a summative report for children in your class.

Planning for formative assessment

Preparation

Before you start to consider assessment in this school placement it will be helpful to review, with your teacher or mentor if possible, your experience of assessment in science. The grid at the end of Assessment and recording in science, Chapter 4 (**page 87**) is a useful way to do this.

You could consider the following questions:

➲ Which approaches to assessment have you found to be both valuable and manageable?
➲ Which assessment methods have you not yet used? Are there any assessment methods that you feel you ought to be including in your practice?
➲ Which of these assessment methods could also be used for diagnostic assessment? Do you need to develop any other assessment techniques for diagnostic purposes?
➲ Which of these assessment methods could also be used for summative assessment? Do you need to develop any other assessment techniques for summative purposes?

Task

Having had these discussions, you should now be in a position to consider how you can build a range of aspects of assessment into your planning for science teaching.

What ideas can you think of in response to each of these headings?

➲ Formative assessment methods that you have not yet used so that you extend your expertise in assessment.

⊃ Suitable assessment methods for children whose home language is not English and who are not yet fluent in English.

⊃ Suitable assessment methods for children with Special Educational Needs who may be low achievers in science.

⊃ Assessment methods that provide sufficient challenge for children who are high achievers in science.

⊃ Assessment of children's scientific skills as well as their scientific knowledge and understanding.

⊃ When and how teacher intervention might occur in response to what you learn through assessment.

Evaluation and follow up
How can you include some of the above in your plans? Don't try to do all of them simultaneously! Be selective, and try out one or two of these aspects of assessment at a time. If it is possible, you should discuss your planning for assessment with the class teacher.

Policy on summative assessment

Preparation
Obtain a copy of the school's assessment policy.

What guidance does it give about how and when summative assessment should take place?
What guidance does it give about recording children's achievements in science?
What guidance does it give about reporting children's achievements in science?
What are the implications for you in planning for summative assessment in science?

Task
Discuss with the class teacher your role in relation to summative assessment, as described in the policy. Is there any national testing happening while you are in the school? What contribution can you make to producing reports for parents for the children in your class?

Evaluation and follow up
Prepare reports for parents if this is acceptable.

Recording assessment judgements

Preparation
Use the National Curriculum level descriptions to help you to organise a systematic record of the children's achievements in science, in consultation with the class teacher. Use this throughout your placement to build up a profile of the children in your class.

Task
At the end of a topic make a summative judgement about the children's progress in science. You may feel the need to use a specific activity or test to help you to do this. Discuss the children's overall progress with your class teacher and/or with the science co-ordinator, then write a report against the National Curriculum level descriptions for the children concerned.

Evaluation and follow up
Review your practice in assessment and recording achievement. Identify areas where you feel that further experience or awareness will be helpful. Try to include these in your future planning so as to increase your expertise and awareness.

Review how you have used the assessment information that you have obtained. What difference has it made to your planning and teaching? Has it led to more constructive and purposeful oral or written feedback? Have your interventions been more focused and more purposeful as a result of the information you have?

Consider how to involve children more in self-assessment. You could review the opportunities for assessment that arose in your school placement and consider how self-assessment might have been built into your approach to assessment.

Harlen, W (2000a) *The teaching of science in primary schools* (3rd Edition). London: David Fulton, Chapters 22–3.
Harlen, W (2000b) *Teaching, learning and assessing science 5–12*. London: Paul Chapman, Chapter 13.
Keogh, B and Naylor, S (2000) 'Assessment in the early years', in M de Boo (ed.) *Science 3–6: laying the foundations in the early years*, pp. 48–56. Hatfield: ASE.

Schilling, M (1998) 'KS2 standard tests in science', in R Sherrington (ed.) *ASE guide to primary science education*, pp.130–33. Hatfield: ASE.

Sharp, J, Peacock, G, Johnsey, R, Simon, S and Smith, R (2002) *Primary science: teaching theory and practice*. Exeter: Learning Matters.

Your achievements

Now that you have completed these activities you should be able to:

⮩ review the school's policy on summative assessment and understand your role in relation to this;
⮩ plan for diagnostic, formative and summative assessments;
⮩ use appropriate assessment strategies in your teaching;
⮩ record children's progress;
⮩ report on children's progress using the level descriptions from the National Curriculum.

Chapter 5   Other aspects of science education

Link to Professional Standards for QTS

The activities in this section address the following Standards for the award of QTS:

1.1; 1.2; 1.3; 1.7; 2.4; 3.1.1; 3.1.2; 3.3.1; 3.3.3; 3.3.6; 3.14.

Introduction

This section invites you to develop a research-based perspective on your professional practice. If you have completed the section on Classroom management, organisation and resources, you will have already tried this in a small way. A research-based perspective means that you continue to try to improve your teaching by reflecting systematically on what happens in your lessons. When things go wrong you try to identify the cause of the problem and modify your teaching, so that next time is better than last time. When things go well you try to identify what contributed to the success of your lesson and to include these 'success factors' in your teaching, so that next time is as good as last time. In this way you can expect your professional awareness to grow, your expertise to increase and your teaching to gradually improve over time. The hallmark of highly successful teachers is that they never stop trying to improve their teaching and that they are never satisfied with their current performance. Although they may not talk about adopting a research-based perspective, this is how they have become as good as they are.

Your research may focus on issues related to child motivation and thinking skills to see if you can find ways to improve motivation by improving your practice.

Illustration of a research-based approach

Suppose that you have read about girls tending to take a back seat in practical activities and you decide that this seems very plausible. When you review your own practice you realise that some of the girls (not all of them) always seem to do the recording but you can't recall them being involved very often in hands-on activity or in using thinking skills. You decide that if this is continually repeated then the girls' confidence is likely to diminish and that they may become reluctant to engage in practical activities themselves.

You confirm your tentative evaluation during your next science lesson. It seems obvious that some of the girls are avoiding the hands-on activities and settle quickly into a routine of recording what the other children do.

You consider a number of possible approaches including:

- ➲ rearranging the groups;
- ➲ talking to the girls about what roles they take on;
- ➲ talking to the more dominant children about what roles they take on;
- ➲ managing the roles that children take on;
- ➲ getting them to do the investigation individually;
- ➲ trying to find practical activities that you think the girls will enjoy.

You decide to positively manage the roles that children take on. You therefore plan to identify specific roles within the next investigation, looking at thermal insulators. These include getting the necessary resources, setting up the investigation, taking temperature readings, recording the readings, drawing a chart and putting the results in a class table. Since each group will be looking at three or four different materials, you plan to get groups to agree individual roles and then switch roles each time they look at a different material.

This goes reasonably according to plan when you teach the lesson. Some children try to manipulate the roles that they take on, but you are alert to this and lend a hand to ensure that individuals do actually take on different roles.

After the lesson you can see that the girls you were concerned about have each been involved in a variety of roles and seemed to enjoy the experience. On reflection you can see the value of being explicit about the different roles involved in activities on a more regular basis. You decide to identify roles more frequently and to use a number of strategies to share out the roles, including taking turns, random selection by drawing names out of a hat and employing the children choosing roles. This would enable you to have conversations with the class about the value of the different roles and the different skills involved, getting them thinking more about their own learning.

Suggestions for further reading about research in science and classroom-based research are given at the end of this section.

Using an action research approach

Preparation
Read the section on Other aspects of science education in Chapter 2 (**page 34**).

Now think about your own planning and teaching of science in terms of child motivation, inclusion and development of thinking skills. Consider questions such as:

- In what ways might children be disadvantaged, alienated, ignored or stereotyped?
- How do you avoid presenting a stereotypical, white, male, Eurocentric, fact-dominated view of science?
- How do children appear to respond to your science teaching in terms of their involvement, concentration, collaboration, enthusiasm and persistence?
- To what extent are children given real cognitive challenges that require them to use and develop their thinking skills?

Are there issues in your science teaching, or aspects of children's responses, that you feel you ought to address? In other words, where do you feel you could be more successful or where do you feel that children could be more highly involved?

Task
Now you are ready to carry out your research.

1 Select one of the issues that you have identified.
2 Consider *possible* ways in which your planning and teaching might be improved.
3 Select one or more strategies that seem most likely to lead to a positive improvement.
4 Incorporate this strategy (or these strategies) into your planning.
5 Consider how you might tell whether the strategy has been successful. This may require you to look for specific indicators of success, or possibly to get a colleague to observe you teaching and look for specific indicators of success.
6 Implement your selected strategy in your next science lesson.
7 Consider how successful your selected strategy was. (If it wasn't particularly successful, consider whether and how you might be able to modify it to make it more successful. Alternatively, choose one of the other possible strategies that you identified earlier.)
8 Rethink your planning to incorporate this new strategy.
9 Implement your selected strategy in your teaching and consider how successful your selected strategy is.
10 Do this for as long as necessary until you know that your teaching has improved, then consider how you might be able to build your successful strategy into your planning and teaching on a long-term basis.
11 Then choose another issue and go through the process again!

Evaluation and follow up
Discuss your findings with your teacher or mentor. Now you have begun to engage in research-based practice you should think of building this in as a strategy in your teaching. It is also worth thinking more broadly about engagement in research. You may be able to take part in local or national research projects, put in a bid for practitioner research funding or register for a higher qualification. The data that you have collected as part of this activity could be the start of this process. If you feel that you have found out anything that may be of interest to other colleagues, the Association for Science Education's Primary Science Review would be very happy to consider your ideas for publication. You can visit the website for further information: www.ase.org.uk

Bell, J (1993) *Doing your research project.* Buckingham: Open University.
Harlen, W (1999) *Effective teaching of science: a review of research.* Edinburgh: SCRE.
Hopkins, D (1985) *A teacher's guide to classroom research.* Milton Keynes: Open University.
Monk, M and Osborne, J (2000) *Good practice in science teaching: what research has to say.* Buckingham: Open University.

Your achievements

Now that you have completed these activities you should be able to:

⊃ use an action research approach to identify issues related to your teaching;
⊃ use the research to help you to respond to issues in your science teaching.

An important part of professional development is review and action planning. Now that you have completed the Extending your Skills phase of your development as a teacher you should review what actions you need to take as you move on towards your first teaching appointment.

For the activities that you have completed in this chapter, you can use the grid below to summarise your professional development. We recommend that you complete this grid in discussion with your teacher, tutor or other professional colleague. In preparation for the discussion tick the activities that you have completed (we have listed them separately although it is likely that you will have carried them out as one whole experience). Rate your confidence level roughly from low to high. Through discussion you need to decide on the actions you need to take to develop your understanding. These will feed into your Career Entry Profile (see Chapter 6 Moving On)

If you are feeling less confident then using some of the strategies above will be essential to ensure that you are able to make progress. These areas are likely to contribute to the targets in your Career Entry Profile.

Your training provider is likely to want to check that you have acquired the appropriate evidence of your achievement of the Standards.

Extending your Skills – review and action planning grid

Theme	Activities	Confidence Low → High			Action
1 Progression in ideas	• Learning how to respond to children's misconceptions				
2 Teaching and learning strategies	• Learning about a range of strategies for teaching science				
3 Teaching practical science	• Teaching children how to engage in critical thinking				
4 Classroom management and resourcing	• Reviewing a range of management strategies in science				
5 Planning and teaching science	• Extending your management skills				
6 Children communicating science	• Looking at communicating science through literacy and numeracy				
7 Assessment and recording	• Using summative and formative assessment in science				
8 Other aspects of science education	• Carry out classroom-based research to consider inclusion and thinking skills				

Chapter 6   Moving On

The final part of this book is about reviewing your experiences as a science teacher. There is one final activity to complete before the book is concluded and you move on into your career as a teacher.

Preparation

In Chapter 2 we met Mrs Martineau and her class. Throughout the book we have seen further evidence of how she has addressed some of the key issues in teaching science to ensure that her practice is effective. If you now return to Chapter 2, **page 8**, you will recall that you reflected on her practice using indicators of effective science teaching. It is now time for you to look at your own practice using the same criteria. This will enable you to reflect on your achievements to date and to identify your individual strengths and areas for further development within your professional practice. This will be the start of a continuing process that is designed to support your professional development throughout your career. It will encourage you to set high expectations for yourself and continually update and improve your practice.

Task

Use the table on **page 118** to reflect on your own teaching. In the first column, try to be honest about the extent to which you achieved each criterion in your teaching.

Next, decide how confident you are that you can achieve this consistently in your teaching. There may be times when you feel that you have good evidence of achievement but your confidence is still low because of the context in which it was achieved or the support that you were given.

Finally, where your achievement and/or confidence is fairly low, consider each of the themes that have been addressed within this book to decide what aspect of your teaching may need to be developed in order to improve your practice. Remember, as always, to talk about this activity with professional colleagues as appropriate, including:

➲ your tutor;
➲ your class teacher;
➲ your mentor;
➲ your trainee colleagues.

Some indicators of good practice												
Indicators of good practice in science	Was this illustrated in your teaching at any time? What evidence do you have of this?	Level of confidence in being able to achieve this in your teaching Low → High			Which aspect of your teaching might be developed to improve practice in this area?							
					Progression	Teaching strategies	Practical science	Management	Planning	Communication	Assessment	Other aspects
A clear sense of purpose to the activity												
Children actively engaged, thinking as well as doing												
Activities are accessible to the children (e.g. language used, concepts involved)												
Activity is responsive to the children's own ideas												
A motivating stimulus for activities												
Teacher uses productive questions that lead on to further enquiry												
A climate of enquiry – children are encouraged to ask their own questions												
Children encouraged to act as independent learners												
Teacher helps the children to learn how to investigate												
Teacher has suitable knowledge of the subject and how to teach it												

Source: Adapted from Keogh, B. and Naylor, S. (1997) *Starting points for science*. Sandbach: Millgate House.

Evaluation and follow up

The end of the training process is identifying targets for further growth and the completion of your Career Entry Profile (CEP). This will be produced in consultation with your training provider. The CEP will be used throughout your induction year to review your progress and set an agenda for your continuing professional development. The CEP has space for only a small number of achievements and targets. It is possible that you will decide not to have a specific target for science on your CEP. However, the targets that you set now will enable you to discuss science-specific development with your induction mentor and science co-ordinator in your new school.

Use the grid above and your completed needs assessment grids from Chapter 2 to help you to complete the review sheet opposite.

Review of progress in science			
	Strengths	Targets	Action (where needed)
Progression in ideas QTS Standards			
Teaching and learning strategies QTS Standards			
Teaching practical science QTS Standards			
Classroom management, organisation and resources QTS Standards			
Planning and teaching science QTS Standards			
Children communicating and recording science QTS Standards			
Assessment and recording in science QTS Standards			
Other aspects of science education QTS Standards			

Further professional development

Opportunities for further professional development will be influenced by local and government priorities during your teaching life. However, you should also take a strong lead in determining your own professional development needs and in agreeing how these will be addressed.

At the end of your induction year you will be assessed by the head teacher against the Induction Standards and you will also have to demonstrate that you have continued to meet the Standards for the Award of Qualified Teacher Status in an employment context.

You need to be clear about the arrangements for your induction period in terms of the procedures, the levels of support available to you and your own roles and responsibilities. The details of these are available in the booklet *Into Induction* as well as on the TTA website.

The evidence you collect throughout this year can be used to begin your Professional Development Record. This should record your progress, performance and professional development needs, which will be reviewed on an annual basis through the performance management process. This process is one aspect of a DfES initiative to encourage and support teachers in continuing to update and share their knowledge, skills and practice in order to enhance children's learning. The DfES has provided a framework that maps the different standards that apply at different stages of a teacher's career. It also includes ten dimensions of teaching and leadership that exist within a school and you are encouraged to chart your progress against these as you move through your career. It is important for you to recognise your areas of expertise and achievements as well as identifying your development needs. The dimensions are:

- ➲ knowledge and understanding;
- ➲ planning and setting expectations;
- ➲ teaching and managing children's learning;
- ➲ assessment and evaluation;
- ➲ children's achievements;
- ➲ relations with parents and the wider community;
- ➲ managing your own performance and development;
- ➲ managing and developing staff and other adults;
- ➲ managing resources;
- ➲ strategic leadership.

As well as the support that may be available to you in the school you will also be able to take advantage of other continuing professional development opportunities such as:

⮑ Association for Science Education regional and annual meetings and courses;
⮑ courses offered by LEAs;
⮑ courses offered by professional organisations such as the Institute of Physics;
⮑ special initiatives supported by professional organisations, industry or government;
⮑ commercially produced resources;
⮑ professional reading;
⮑ registering for a degree module from your local university or the Open University;
⮑ websites – these are regularly updated and provide opportunities to access new resources and to gain access to ideas from other teachers.

One of the best sources of professional help is the Association for Science Education (ASE). Through this organisation you can gain access to teachers of primary science and to a wide network of expertise in the field of science education. You should check if the school is a member of the Association for Science Education. If it is, you should ensure that you gain access to their publications and to information about courses and other events. Alternatively, you could join the organisation yourself. We would particularly recommend this if you are the science co-ordinator. You can obtain all the information you need from their website: www.ase.org.uk

Finally …

We are aware that many trainees start their training very wary of teaching primary science. We also know that by the end of their training many of those trainees have developed a love for teaching science and have developed a growing confidence in their own understanding of science and how it can be taught. Generally this is because they discover that science learning can be different from what they experienced as learners, and have seen science as more dynamic and exciting than they had anticipated. When they see a child who has struggled with literacy and numeracy suddenly blossom in science then they realise the value of including science in the primary school curriculum.

We hope that this book has helped you to develop a love for teaching science.

Bibliography

Progression in ideas

DfEE (1998) Circular 4/98, *Teaching: high status, high standards*. London: DfEE.

Driver, R, Guesne, E, and Tiberghien, A (eds) (1985) *Children's ideas in science*. Milton Keynes: Open University.

Driver, R, Squires, A, Rushworth, P, and Wood-Robinson, V (1994) *Making sense of secondary science*. London: Routledge.

Harlen, W (2000) *The teaching of science in primary schools* (3rd Edition). London: David Fulton.

Johnsey, R, Peacock, G, Sharp, J and Wright, G (2002) *Primary science: knowledge and understanding* (2nd Edition). Exeter: Learning Matters.

Naylor, S and Keogh, B (1998) 'Progression and differentiation in science: some specific strategies', in A Cross and G Peet (eds) *Teaching science in the primary school: Book 2,* pp. 44–58. Plymouth: Northcote House.

Naylor, S and Keogh, B (2000) *Concept cartoons in science education*. Sandbach: Millgate House.

Peacock, G (1998) *QTS. Science for primary teachers: an audit and self-study guide*. London: Letts.

Sharp, J and Byrne, J (2001) *Achieving QTS. Primary science audit and test*. Exeter: Learning Matters.

Sharp, J, Peacock, G, Johnsey, R, Simon, S and Smith, R (2002) *Primary science: teaching theory and practice*. Exeter: Learning Matters.

Various authors (1993) *Nuffield Primary Science Teachers' Guides*. London: Collins Educational.

Watt, D (1998) 'Children's learning of scientific concepts', in R Sherrington (ed.) *ASE guide to primary science education*, pp. 51–62. Hatfield: ASE.

Website
Science Line: www.sciencenet.org.uk

Teaching and learning strategies

Asoko, H and de Boo, M (2001) *Analogies and illustrations: representing ideas in primary science*. Hatfield: ASE.

BJSE (1992) Special issue on differentiation of the *British Journal of Special Education*, 19(1).

Dickinson, C and Wright, J (1993) *Differentiation: a practical handbook of classroom strategies*. Coventry: NCET.

Goldsworthy, A and Holmes, M (1999) *Teach it! Do it! Let's get to it!* Hatfield: ASE.

Harlen, W (2000) *The teaching of science in primary schools* (3rd Edition). London: David Fulton, Chapters 7, 9 and 10.

Naylor, S and Keogh, B (1998) 'Differentiation', in R Sherrington (ed.) *ASE guide to primary science education,* pp. 140–7. Hatfield: ASE.

Naylor, S and Keogh, B (2000) *Concept cartoons in science education*. Sandbach: Millgate House.

NIAS (1995) *The differentiation book*. Northants: NIAS.

Smith, A (1995) *Accelerated learning in the classroom*. Stafford: Network Educational Press.

Various authors (1993) *Nuffield Primary Science Teachers' Guides*. London: Collins Educational.

Website
Association for Science Education: www.ase.org.uk

Teaching practical science

de Boo, M (1999) *Enquiring children, challenging teaching: investigating primary science*. Buckingham: Open University.

Feasey, R (1998) 'Effective questioning in science', in R Sherrington (ed.) *ASE guide to primary science education*, pp. 156–167. Hatfield: ASE.

Fisher, R (1990) *Teaching children to think*. London: Simon & Schuster.

Goldsworthy, A and Feasey, R (1997) *Making sense of primary science investigations* (2nd Edition). Hatfield: ASE.

Goldsworthy, A and Holmes, M (1999) *Teach it! Do it! Let's get to it!* Hatfield: ASE.

Harlen, W (1998) 'The last ten years; the next ten years', in R Sherrington (ed.) *ASE guide to primary science education*, pp. 23–33. Hatfield: ASE.

Harlen, W (2000) *The teaching of science in primary schools* (3rd Edition). London: David Fulton, especially Chapters 9, 10, 13 and 20.

Jarvis, T (1995) 'What shall we put in the fruit salad? Developing investigative thinking and skills in children', in J Moyles (ed.) *Beginning teaching, beginning learning*, pp. 115–28. Buckingham: Open University.

Ratcliffe, M (1998) 'The purposes of science education', in R Sherrington (ed.) *ASE guide to primary science education*, pp. 3–12. Hatfield: ASE.

Classroom management, organisation and resources

ASE (2001) *Be safe* (3rd Edition). Hatfield: ASE.

Feasey, R (1998) *Primary science equipment*. Hatfield: ASE.

Harlen, W (1999) *Effective teaching of science: a review of research*. Edinburgh: SCRE.

Hodson (1998) *Teaching and learning in science*. Buckingham: Open University.

Hollins, M (1998) 'Resources for teaching science', in R Sherrington (ed.) *ASE guide to primary science education*, pp. 206–15. Hatfield: ASE.

Howe, C (1995) 'Learning about physics through peer interaction', in P Murphy, M Selinger, J Bourne and M Briggs (eds) *Subject learning in the primary curriculum*, pp. 197–204. London: Routledge.

SCIcentre (1999) *Primary science classroom organisation* (video). Leicester: University of Leicester and University of Cambridge.

Sharp, J, Peacock, G, Johnsey, R, Simon, S and Smith, R (2002) *Achieving QTS. Primary science: teaching theory and practice*. Exeter: Learning Matters, Chapter 7.

Sjoberg, S (2000) 'Interesting all children in "science for all",' in R Millar, J Leach and J Osborne (eds) *Improving science education*, pp. 167–86. Buckingham: Open University.

Waterson, A (2000) 'Managing the classroom for learning', in K Jacques and R Hyland (eds) *Achieving QTS. Professional studies: primary phase*, pp. 74–92. Exeter: Learning Matters.

Planning and teaching science

DfEE (1999) *The National Curriculum: handbook for primary teachers in England*. London: DfEE/QCA.

Naylor, S and Keogh, B (1998) 'Differentiation', in R Sherrington (ed.) *ASE guide to primary science education*, pp. 140–7. Hatfield: ASE.

QCA (1998) *Science: a scheme of work for Key Stages 1 and 2*. London: QCA.

Sharp, J, Peacock, G, Johnsey, R, Simon, S and Smith, R (2002) *Achieving QTS. Primary science: teaching theory and practice*. Exeter: Learning Matters, Chapter 6.

Children communicating and recording science

Ball, S (1998) 'Science and information technology', in R Sherrington (ed) *ASE guide to primary science education*, pp. 168–74. Hatfield: ASE.

Burton, N (1995) *How to be brilliant at recording in science*. Leamington Spa: Brilliant Publications.

DfEE (1999a) *The National Curriculum: handbook for primary teachers in England*. London: DfEE/QCA.

DfEE (1999b) *The National Numeracy Strategy: framework for teaching mathematics from Reception to Year 6*. London: DfEE.

Feasey, R (1998) *Primary science and literacy*. Hatfield: ASE. Topics 3 and 4 deal specifically with scientific vocabulary.

Feasey, R and Gallear, B (2000) *Primary science and numeracy*. Hatfield: ASE.

Feasey, R and Gallear, B (2001) *Primary science and Information Communication Technology*. Hatfield: ASE.

First Steps (1998) *Writing: resource book*. Australia: Rigby Heinemann.

Harlen, W (2000) *The teaching of science in primary schools* (3rd Edition). London: David Fulton, Chapter 12.

Newton, D (2002) *Talking sense in science*. London: Routledge.

Nuffield Primary Science (1998) *Science and literacy. A guide for primary teachers*. London: Collins Educational.

QCA (1998) *Science: a scheme of work for Key Stages 1 and 2*. London: QCA.

Sharp, J, Peacock, G, Johnsey, R, Simon, S and Smith, R (2002) *Primary science: teaching theory and practice*. Exeter: Learning Matters, Chapters 3 and 9.

Assessment and recording in science

Black, P and Wiliam, D (1998) *Inside the black box*. London: Kings College.

Feasey, R (1998) 'Effective questioning in science', in R Sherrington (ed.) *ASE guide to primary science education*. Hatfield: ASE.

Harlen, W (ed.) (1985) *Primary science: taking the plunge*. London: Heinemann.

Harlen, W (2000a) *The teaching of science in primary schools* (3rd Edition). London: David Fulton.

Harlen, W (2000b) *Teaching, learning and assessing science 5–12*. London: Paul Chapman.

Hayes, P (1998) 'Assessment in the classroom', in R Sherrington (ed) *ASE guide to primary science education*, pp. 125–9. Hatfield: ASE.

Keogh, B and Naylor, S (2000) 'Assessment in the early years', in M de Boo (ed.) *Science 3–6: laying the foundations in the early years*, pp. 48–56. Hatfield: ASE.

Naylor, S and Keogh, B (2000) *Concept cartoons in science education*. Sandbach: Millgate House.

Schilling, M (1998) 'KS2 standard tests in science', in R Sherrington (ed.) *ASE guide to primary science education*. Hatfield: ASE.

Sharp, J, Peacock, G, Johnsey, R, Simon, S and Smith, R (2002) *Primary science: teaching theory and practice*. Exeter: Learning Matters.

White, R and Gunstone, R (1992) *Probing understanding*. London: Falmer.

Other aspects of science education

Bell, J (1993) *Doing your research project*. Buckingham: Open University.

DfEE (1999) *The National Curriculum: handbook for primary teachers in England*. London: DfEE/QCA.

Fisher, R (1990) *Teaching children to think*. London: Basil Blackwell.

Harlen, W (1999) *Effective teaching of science: a review of research*. Edinburgh: SCRE.

Hopkins, D (1985) *A teacher's guide to classroom research*. Milton Keynes: Open University.

Monk, M and Osborne, J (2000) *Good practice in science teaching: what research has to say*. Buckingham: Open University.

NACCCE (1999) *All our Futures: creativity, culture and education* (the *Robinson Report*). London: DfEE.

Peet, G (1998) 'Equal opportunities', in A Cross and G Peet (eds) *Teaching science in the primary school: Book 2*, pp. 59–74. Plymouth: Northcote House.

Ratcliffe, M and Lock, R (1998) 'Opinions and values in learning science', in R Sherrington (ed.) *ASE guide to primary science education*, pp. 83–90. Hatfield: ASE.

Reiss, M (1998) 'Science for all', in R Sherrington (ed.) *ASE guide to primary science education*, pp. 34–43. Hatfield: ASE.

Smith, A (1995) *Accelerated learning in the classroom*. Stafford: Network Educational Press.

Thorp, S (1991) *Race, equality and science teaching*. Hatfield: ASE.

Woolnough, B (1994) *Effective science teaching*. Milton Keynes: Open University.

Websites

Association for Science Education: www.ase.org.uk

Science Line: www.sciencenet.org.uk

Teacher Training Agency: www.canteach.gov.uk

Index

ability, grouping by, 20
action research approach, 114
activities, to make children's ideas
        evident, 11
analogies, in teaching, 14–15
analysis, classroom management
        strategies, 103
assessment
    inclusive approach, 35
    planning for, 105
    and recording in science
        developing your skills, 85–7
        extending your skills, 110–12
        getting started, 57–9
        guidance and needs analysis,
        31–3
attitudes, scientific, 18
aural learners, 13

Be Safe, 21

children communicating and recording
        science
    developing your skills, 82–4
    extending your skills, 107–9
    getting started, 54–6
    guidance and needs analysis, 27–30
classroom layout, 20
classroom management, organisation
        and resources
    developing your skills, 75–7
    extending your skills, 101–3
    getting started, 49–50
    guidance and needs analysis, 19–21
closed questions, 31
cognitive challenges, 35
communicating see children
        communicating and recording
        in science
concept cartoons, 32
concept maps, 32
consolidation, progression in
        understanding, 10
constructivist approach, 9
critical thinking, developing, 100
cultural development, 35

decision-making, scientific
        investigations, 99
demonstration, 14
developing your skills, 6
    assessment and recording in science,
        85–7
    children communicating and
        recording science, 82–4

classroom management, organisation
        and resources, 75–7
    introduction, 65–6
    other aspects of education, 88–9
    planning and teaching science, 78–81
    progression in ideas, 67–9
    teaching and learning strategies,
        70–1
    teaching practical science, 72–4
differentiation, 13
    matching activities to learning needs,
        79, 80
    special needs, 14, 96, 97
drawings, communication through, 28

evaluation
    classroom management, 76–7, 102
    encouraging and developing, 100
    formative assessment, 86
    linking planning and, 105–6
    recording and communicating
        strategies, 83, 84
    teaching strategies, 45
extending your skills, 6
    assessment and recording in science,
        110–12
    children communicating and
        recording science, 107–9
    classroom management, organisation
        and resources, 101–3
    introduction, 91–2
    other aspects of science education,
        113–15
    planning and teaching science,
        104–6
    progression in ideas, 93–5
    teaching and learning strategies,
        96–7
    teaching practical science, 98–100

fair testing, 72
formative assessment
    comparing approaches, 86
    planning, 87, 110–11
    strategies for, 32–3

gender
    assessment, 35
    grouping by, 20
    practical investigations, 34–5
getting started, 5
    assessment and recording in science,
        57–9
    children communicating and
        recording science, 54–6

classroom management, organisation and resources, 49–50
introduction, 39–40
other aspects of science education, 60–2
planning and teaching science, 51–3
progression in ideas, 41–2
teaching and learning strategies, 43–5
teaching practical science, 46–8
good practice
indicators of, 118
science teaching, 8
groupings, 20
guidance and needs analysis
assessment and recording in science, 31–3
children communicating and recording science, 27–30
classroom management, organisation and resources, 19–21
conclusion, 37–8
introduction, 2, 5–8
other aspects of science education, 34–6
planning and teaching science, 22–4
progression in ideas, 9–12
teaching and learning strategies, 13–16
teaching practical science, 17–18

health and safety, 21
hypothesising, 100

ICT see information and communications technology
ideas
grouping by, 20
recording and communicating, 28–9, 55
see also progression in ideas
illustrations, in teaching, 14–15
images, in science, 35, 60–1
inclusion
language used in science, 35
National Curriculum, 34
individual training plans
developing your skills, 65
getting started, 39
information and communications technology (ICT)
communicating ideas, 29
training children to use, 96
initial teacher training, 1
intervention strategies, developing, 94
investigations
decision-making, 99
practical, 34–5, 75
systematic, 17
investigative skills
planning, 100
progression in, 98–9

kinaesthetic learners, 13

language
children's scientific, 27
influence on inclusion, 35

learning
objectives
identifying, 23
matching activities to, 78, 80
planning for, 105
see also teaching and learning strategies
lesson plans, 23–4, 25f, 51–2, 80
lessons, effective management of, 101
literacy, 29, 107–8
long-term planning, 23

mathematical equipment, training in use of, 15, 96, 97
mathematical skills, 29
medium-term planning, 23
misconceptions
identifying, 68
responding to, 94
models, in teaching, 14–15, 70–1
moral development, 35
motivation, 34, 44, 61
moving on, 117–20

National Curriculum, 22–3, 29, 34
National Curriculum for Initial Teacher Training, 9
national tests, 33
Nuffield Primary Science Teachers' Guides, 10, 11
numeracy, 29, 108–9

observation
of children, 46
classroom organisation and management, 49–50
of recording and communicating, 83
of teacher strategy, 44
open questions, 31
organisation see classroom management, organisation and resources
other aspects of science education
developing your skills, 88–9
extending your skills, 113–15
getting started, 60–2
guidance and needs analysis, 34–6
outdoor visits, 15, 96, 97

people, to involve in needs analysis, 37
person-centred questions, 31
planning
tasks
addressing key issues, 61
formative assessment, 87, 110–11
investigative skills, 100
practical activities, 47, 75
science lessons, 52, 68, 84
small group activity, 44–5
and teaching science
developing your skills, 78–81
extending your skills, 104–6
getting started, 51–3
guidance and needs analysis, 22–4
plenaries, 16
practical investigations, 34–5, 75

predictions, making, 73
priming, 15
process skills, 17
productive questions, 31–2
professional development, 119–20
Professional Standards
    assessment and recording in science,
        57, 85, 110
    children communicating and
        recording science, 54, 82, 107
    classroom management, organisation
        and resources, 49, 75, 101
    evidence of meeting, 3
    other aspects of science education,
        60, 88, 113
    planning and teaching science, 51, 78,
        104
    progression in ideas, 41, 67, 93
    Qualified Teacher Status, 1, 2
    teaching and learning strategies, 43,
        70, 96
    teaching practical science, 46, 72, 98
Programmes of Study, 22
progress, review of, 119
progression in ideas
    developing your skills, 67–9
    extending your skills, 93–5
    getting started, 41–2
    guidance and needs analysis, 9–12

Qualification and Curriculum Authority
        (QCA), 23
Qualified Teacher Status (QTS), 1, 2
Qualifying to Teach, 1
questioning, assessment, 31–2, 32
questions
    identifying types of, 57
    including in planning, 79
    raising, 73
    using in teaching, 58

recording
    assessment judgements, 111
    see also assessment and recording in
        science; children communicating
        and recording science
regression, progression in
        understanding, 10
research see scientific enquiry
research-based approach, to science
        education, 113–14
resources, organisation of, 20–1
responding
    to children's ideas, 11
    to misconceptions, 94
risk assessments, 21
role models, 16

Schemes of Work, 10, 11, 23, 42
school policy

reviewing, 88–9
summative assessment, 111
science education see other aspects of
        science education
scientific enquiry
    mathematical skills, 29
    National Curriculum, 22
    planning task, 75
    recommended structure, 17
    scientific attitudes, 18
    thinking skills, 35
    using secondary sources, 14
scientific equipment, training in use of,
        15, 96, 97
secondary sources, research using, 14
sessions, introducing, 15
skills
    progression of ideas, 10
    scientific, 17
small group activity, 20, 44–5
social development, 35
special needs, differentiation, 14, 96, 97
spiritual development, 35
standards see Professional Standards
subject knowledge, 67
subject-centred questions, 31
summative assessment, 111
summative judgements, 33
systematic investigations, 17

teaching
    effectively, 6–8
    investigative skills, 100
    and learning strategies
        developing your skills, 70–1
        extending your skills, 96–7
        getting started, 43–5
        guidance and needs analysis,
            13–16
    practical science
        developing your skills, 72–4
        extending your skills, 98–100
        getting started, 46–8
        guidance and needs analysis,
            17–18
    see also planning and teaching
        science
telling/instructing, 14
terminology, using scientific, 27–8, 54
thinking skills, 35, 89
training, use of scientific equipment, 15,
        96, 97

unproductive questions, 31–2

visitors, 15, 96, 97
visual learners, 13
vocabulary see terminology

whole class involvement, 19